A

Soldier's

Progress

Andrew B. Horval Jr.
U.S. Army Master Sergeant Retired
1994-2016
Soldier for Life and Life Eternal
[LF6]

LF6 Memoir

This memoir edition is self-published and edited by the author. Please forgive any and all formatting and grammar errors that have been overlooked during the proofreading process. The author has a Bachelor of Science in Business Administration with Graduate Level Theological education, not an English/Literary Arts major or graduate with an intention of winning a literary award. The sole intention of this book is so that those who cross paths with the author's thoughts and ministry may have a better understanding of the framework and history that has molded his overall ideology and faith. It is also a testimony for my children, grandchildren, and their children etc.

Personal full names are mostly omitted for privacy. Respect, grace, and room for repentance for those who may have erred while crossing paths with the author has been afforded. Names omitted do not necessarily imply questionable characters. The omission may solely be for the sake of privacy.

First of all, I would like to dedicate this memoir to my LORD and Savior Jesus Christ on the 25th year of my salvation, 23rd year of marriage, 21st/20th/17th/12th years of our children, and 10th year of The Soldier's Sanctuary. Without Him I would not know God and I would not know my beautiful wife Lin. My wife and I are truly blessed and count it a privilege to walk this journey called life together. It is my prayer that each of our four children (Judah, Jesse, Jacky-Lin, and Larry) that God has richly blessed us with will have the same peace and understanding in their own lives and for generations to come for the glory of God our Father and His Kingdom.

This is the LORD'S doing; it is marvellous in our eyes.
Psalms 118:23

Matthew 8:8-10 The centurion answered and said, Lord, I am not worthy that thou shouldest come under my roof: but speak the word only, and my servant shall be healed. For I am a man under authority, having soldiers under me: and I say to this man, Go, and he goeth; and to another, Come, and he cometh; and to my servant, Do this, and he doeth it. When Jesus heard it, he marvelled, and said to them that followed, Verily I say unto you, I have not found so great faith, no, not in Israel.

Lightfighter- Fights for the light and travels light.
Six- Number of man who falls short of the glory of God and the military call sign of a commander
[**LF6**]

Matthew 27:54 Now when the centurion, and they that were with him, watching Jesus, saw the earthquake, and those things that were done, they feared greatly, saying, Truly this was the Son of God.

TABLE OF CONTENTS

FORWARD

Those who do not know me and that may happen upon this memoir may choose to look me up on social media. Do not count on it! My social media presence is very intermittent, sporadic, and unpredictable. I have appeared and then disappeared over the years. Lately, the disappearances have increased in length and will eventually lead to permanent disappearance one way or the other. For years, my internet handle has been Lightfighter Six [LF6] and the following is a collaboration of messages (in bold) I have delivered as the founding pastor of The Soldier's Sanctuary which was founded in 2008. These INCOMING!!! messages and more are all archived on my website.

Social media is a tool if not used correctly will leave us **Thirsty**. Social media and I do not get along and when we cross paths I come to publish the truth and I go to refocus on face to face efforts and relationships. You know the people we talk to on the phone and see on a day to day basis. I have come to the realization that we can only help those who want to be helped and the **Micro-Blogging, Micro- Intellect, Zombie Culture** does not want to be helped for the most part. They just wander from profile to profile seeing what death they can feed upon, continuing to look through a **Dark Glass** where they argue about the **Evil of Guns** and the **Gunslingers** instead of the evil in their hearts. When I post, I post knowing that I can not help the Zombie; but, I know there are those looking for a **Tree of Hope**. I post for them and the one who answers and defines the question, **What is Love**?

Honestly, there is enough of hate and death's stink in the

national headline news and everyday real life to deal with and process let alone a never ending news feed from strangers, marketeers, and **Potlickers** who could care less about us. You do not have to look very deep to see that those with money buy followers, likes, and subscribers so that they can fool the masses into accepting their fake personas. I do not want any part of it! I am treading upon the **Validated Bridge** which leads to the King and **Father of Glory** and not the **King of Pride**. I am not looking for followers, I am looking for others to follow Jesus with me. I am not looking to make a name for myself, I am looking to proclaim the NAME that is above all names.

I want to focus on life and not death and all of its **Sin Babies** which flow from the **Pandora Box** of greed, pride, and lust...all of which should stay in the **Belly of Hell**. Yes! I will address the awful realities of death, but I want to live life in **Truth**. Speaking of life and death, on **October 31, 1993** the Lord saved me. **I AM** what I am today because of what the Lord did for me on that day. He brought me from death unto life. He put me on **The Bus** of eternal life and shifted me from a **Fear of Dog** (world and death) to the fear of God (Life).

Am I better than anyone else because of the awesome transformation that has occurred in my life? Absolutely not! I fall short more than I would ever care to admit. I am continually reminded that we are but **Specks** and **Foot Dust**. This is why we need the Lord for every step and every breath we take in this life. We must not forget **Who We Are** and where we come from. Listen! I will fail you, you will fail me, but Jesus will never fail us.

Is my calling better than your calling? Absolutely not! We

are on the same team as Christian brothers and sisters with our own unique spiritual **Fingerprints** and the will of God for each of our lives is a unique as those fingerprints. With God's will comes a measure of faith, so you will not see me comparing my measure with yours. I am just doing my best to carry out the will of God for my life and to help others carry out the will of God for their lives by God's grace. This includes everyone from the pastor to the **Door Greeter**.

I have no interest in **Commercial Christianity** and its **Den of Thieves**. The irony is that the den leaders plaster themselves all over social media and judge each other by their bot follower count while the **Cock Crows**. I am sticking with **God's Gospel and NOT Man's Manuals** which requires **Taking All Commands from the Tower** fully knowing that the **Hogs and Dogs of Hell** exist and will attempt to thwart us. I have learned that these **Wolves in Sheep's Clothing** are not **Saints**. They are **Oxygen Thieves** and **Spotlight Rangers** who are lacking the **Spiritual Balls** to seek God and obey him rather than men.

I want to be the **Soldier of Christ** that God has called me to be. I want to listen to his **Still Small Voice** and follow his **Orders** and his orders alone. I want to fight the good fight **To The Death** and be in tune with **The Real Social Network** that I am called to be a part of and minister to include those who are **The Forsaken** and those in **The Storms of Depression** so that they too may see the **Light of God**. I do not wish to part of the **Symphony of Crickets**, **Gaggle of Gnats**, and **Flattering Lips** that ignore true religion which is to minister to the fatherless, widows, and poor. On the contrary, I want to be a **True Disciple** who is willing to work and share the **Genuine**

Faith Recipe with them and their loved ones. These are the **Grounds of Respect** and love that I want to stand upon.

We must wake up to the fact that we are in a war, a war between the **Kingdoms of Bling** and the Kingdom of God. Sometime we are going to have to **Fix Bayonets** to fight against the religious and political **Establishment Delusion** if we are going to be the **Warriors of Regeneration** that we are called to be. Otherwise we will continually find ourselves under the **Tree of Sorrow** listening for the **Voice in the Wilderness** which is crying out **If My People**. So many are missing out by **18 inches** from finding **Perfect Peace**. They act as if they were the **Persecuted Ones**, but believe me...we have not seen persecution in its purest form.

Sometimes forgiveness **Seventy Times Seven** is in the way, sometimes pride and Selfishness is. Call out to the **Father of Fathers** and know that there is a **Divine Appointment** awaiting you. You too can put on the **Coat of Freedom** and attend the **College of Contentment** as I have. After all there is peace and **Justice for All** which is the **Central Theme**!

The bottom line is that we need to wake up out of our **Deep Sleep** and stop being a **Hostage** of Satan. We need to look in the **Mirror** and be the Men/Women of War and **Lightfighters** that God has called us to be without forgetting there is **No I In Team**. We are just **Pilgrims** following the **Leadership** of God Almighty doing our best to stay in our **Lanes** as member of the **Legions of Liberty**.

Jesus is God, the **Aleph and the Trinity** so **Follow Him** and become the **Sower** that God wants us all to be which is my primary purpose of Social Media. All I am trying to say as a Wise friend has said more than once. The give-a-penny-take-a-penny tray is empty. You and I can not take from it anymore. It is time to start making some **Bank Deposits** for the Glory of God. So if you want to "prophesy" something. **Prophecy This**! It is time to mount up! So let's get on our **War Horses** and fight the good fight.

BORN AGAIN

As a young child Samuel had an encounter with the LORD that he understood very little about at the time. Clearly, the encounter was a sacred spark ignited by the hand of God that would be used for a later fire in Samuel's spiritual life and walk with God. I too experienced these very same sparks as a young child.

1 Samuel 3:4-5 That the LORD called Samuel:
and he answered, Here am I. And he ran unto Eli,
and said, Here am I; for thou calledst me. And he said,
I called not; lie down again. And he went and lay down.

Three years after my birth in 1975 and fifteen years before I would be born again in 1993, I remember riding in the car with my Dad as a three year old and asking, "Dad, can we go to church?" Little did I know at such a young age the LORD was calling me. It is the very first spark of spirituality in my life that I can remember.

Throughout my childhood and teenage years God in his timing would sporadically ignite other sparks by getting my young mind to focus upon him briefly. Some sparks would endure longer than others; nevertheless, they were still sacred sparks that I cherish even unto this day. Sparks that would be even recorded in this book decades later.

The sacred sparks that ignited in my heart as a child are the same type of sparks that I am continually looking for in the lives of my own children, family, friends, and those I interact with on a daily basis. I realize no matter the stage of life they are in that God could very well be calling their name and lighting a spark. As Samuel could not immediately discern the LORD's voice and respond accordingly, I understand God who is long suffering and rich in grace continues to call our name until one day the fire ignites in our souls.

You would not be reading this today if the culmination of sacred sparks in my young life did not reach combustion and explode into flames of fire on the day of my salvation. A fire that I hope and pray God uses to ignite the souls of those I cross paths with starting with my own children.

Proverbs 22:6 Train up a child in the way he should go: and when he is old, he will not depart from it.

It is imperative that we do not ignore the merciful and gracious sacred sparks that God ignites in our hearts throughout our lives. If God's Holy Fire of Love and Grace does not ignite into flames within our souls on this side of eternity, all we have left to experience is God's Holy Fire of Justice and Wrath on the other side. I am just glad and eternally grateful that my story of fire is told on this side.

1 Samuel 3:19 And Samuel grew, and the LORD was with him, and did let none of his words fall to the ground.

Many years ago as a young child in the third grade I sat in a pew and rapidly fire off a series of "Our Father's" and "Hail Mary's" in a repetitive manner. Prior to my "prayerful" event at the pew a priest prescribed a certain amount of the memorized prayers as part of the absolution of my long list of sins as a child. I was quite mischievous.

I followed the prescription just as the priest had ordered, but not without question and doubt. As I sat in the pew I began to meditate upon just exactly what was occurring in that pew. What did the recited prayers accomplish? If they meant very little to me, would they not seem rather insignificant to God?

We did not study the Bible as elementary Catholic students, so I was not aware of Matthew 6:7. Nevertheless, a still small voice spoke to me as I briefly meditated upon my questions and doubt.

Matthew 6:7 But when ye pray, use not vain repetitions, as the heathen do: for they think that they shall be heard for their much speaking.

Since I became a born-again Christian the Hail Mary's were scrapped. Actually, it was a long time before my salvation this type of prayer was recited anyways. However, once I discovered that Jesus is our sole mediator and I had no need for Mary or any other saint to intercede on my behalf these types of prayers were shunned.

1 Timothy 2:5 For there is one God, and one mediator between God and men, the man Christ Jesus;

Not only were these types of prayers shunned, so was the repetitive aspect. Because many do not read the Bible they do not even realize that there is a proclamation preceding the "Our Father" prayer that is recited by millions all across the world.

Matthew 6:9 After this manner therefore pray ye: Our Father which art in heaven, Hallowed be thy name.

"After this manner therefore pray ye," instructs us that the "Our Father" is a model prayer or the framework for the prayer. For instance, in Matthew 6:9 we could spend considerable time praising the name of our Holy God. This expansion of thought and prayer will leave us no room for repetitive reciting of the framework or model of this prayer. We must not forget that the "Our Father" is only a model and framework for genuine heartfelt prayer that does not stop at the framework. The substance of this type of prayer finds itself within and between the lines of the model prayer that God has given us.

Later in the sixth grade I remember sitting in my room finding myself engrossed in a religion book that was assigned for reading at the Catholic elementary school I attended. Particularly, it was the Gospel stories that I was reading that captured my attention. Each story was powerful and had a tremendous attraction that resonated with my mind, heart, and soul. I treasure this memory very much until this day. The Lord knew that one day I would surrender to his will and way within in due time. I am amazed that his Spirit would be so gracious as to light a holy spark here and there in the early days of my life, especially when there was not a whole lot of holy sparks around me.

Divorce

My parents divorced by the time I was 5 years old. Neither of them were outwardly spiritual at all; however, they did take us to church services periodically. It is my continued prayer that each of them would have a solid understanding of the Gospel message and would respond accordingly. Thankfully, they have supported me throughout my career in the Army and have not looked down on the ministry that God has called me to either. Within the past year of this book's completion my Dad made a point to let me know that he is reading and listening to my messages online which means much to me. None of us are perfect and neither are they. I loved them just the same. The family must exercise unconditional love if it is to survive.

Mark 10:11-12 And he saith unto them, Whosoever shall put away his wife, and marry another, committeth adultery against her. And if a woman shall put away her husband, and be married to another, she committeth adultery.

Divorce is ugly and it does not take a book to teach us this. The statistics are staggering! In 2012, according to the United States Census Bureau, roughly 25% of the U.S. population had married two or more times.[1]

Appendix Table E.				
Percentage of Ever-Married Men and Women 15 Years Old and Over That Had Married Two or More Times by State: 2008-20121 (For information on confidentiality protection, sampling error, nonsampling error, and definitions, see www.census.gov/acs/www/Downloads/data_documentation/Accuracy/MultiyearACSAccuracyofData2012.pdf)				
	Percent married two or more times			
State or equivalent	Men		Women	
	Percent	Margin of error2	Percent	Margin of error2
U.S. total.....................	24.8	0.04	24.4	0.04

There is a coordinated Satanic attach on the family that continues to destroy the very basis of our society. By God's grace, I am doing my best to combat against the decline of the sanctity of marriage. As soon as I became licensed by the State of Ohio to solemnize marriages I vowed that I would not marry anyone who was previously divorced or not a professing Born-Again Christian. I would not even marry a great friend of mine, who is also the first charter member outside of my family, when he remarried. However, I still attended, remotely do to my Army commitment at the time, as his best man.

Why such a dogmatic stance? Simply, to make a statement. Even though my childhood was not overly abusive, there were abuses that could have been avoided if divorce was not an option. This is exactly what my wife and I have determined in our own marriage- Divorce is not an option!

[1] U.S. Census Bureau. 2012
https://www.census.gov/data/tables/2012/demo/marriage-and-divorce/acs-30.html

Traditions

Throughout my youthful years I am reminded now as I write this just a few days before Christmas of the solemn church observances of the birth of our Savior. I loved to hear the music flow from the pipe organs. I loved the light that illuminated the sanctuary along with the smell of incense. These are some of the things I even miss today; however, I do not miss the traditions that contradict the Word of God. These would not be the first or last traditions I would come in contact with either that I would reject. Every religious organization that I have come in contact with has inconsistencies and I have since come to the conclusion that there is no perfect church just as there is no perfect person other than Jesus Christ our Lord.

Mark 7:9,13 And he said unto them, Full well ye reject the commandment of God, that ye may keep your own tradition. Making the word of God of none effect through your tradition, which ye have delivered: and many such like things do ye.

I remember attending a church service with a friend whose family started going to church not too long before I went with them. I noticed changes right away but for some reason none of them really registered with me. My friend threw away his Heavy Metal music, which was very strange to me. Even so, I did not dwell on it too much, mainly because I was a teenager thinking about girls and what trouble I could get into. While at the service I remember people going forward to the altar. I did not feel moved to go forward at the time, but I do remember thinking about what had occurred. The experience was soon pushed to the back of my mind and would be filed away for future recollection and contemplation.

High School

I started entertaining thoughts about the Army during my freshman year of High School. One day the recruiters came to our school with some recent graduates from Basic Training. I asked him about what it took to be a warrant officer so I could fly helicopters. He looked at me like I was an idiot and spouted off with something I can not remember intending to blow me off. That did not sit well with me and became just another thought that was filed away for later use. Many years later as an Army recruiter I would realize that the Privates were clueless about career options with the Army and could probably care less about whether or not I personally enlisted.

At this point in my life things at home were not well at all. I just started a job working at a donut shop and was required to start paying rent at home. Growing up there was constant struggle between my stepmother and I. This new job only proved to be another struggle because I was then required to pay $25.00 a week and I was not able to use the wash machine or dryer. This did not sit well with me, so the wheels of my brain began to go into action to develop a plan to circumvent the new fee. I spoke with my co-workers at the time and made a proposal to pay them the $25.00 a week that would include wash machine privileges while staying with them. Surprisingly, they agreed. I them told my Dad about my new plan which he most likely thought I was blowing smoke so he said, "fine! You think you can make it on your own, go!" And go I did, I packed up my goods and remember being loaded down on a cold winter day as I made my way to my new residence.

A few weeks later my Dad got in contact with me and convinced me that it would be in my best interest to live with my Aunt and Uncle. I agreed because in the back of my mind I know it would be best to stay with family. I stayed with them for a short while but because of my behavior I found myself soon after looking for a new place to reside. Ironically, this Uncle would be the same Uncle to lead me to the Lord after he was saved not long after I had left their house.

After leaving my Aunt and Uncle's house I went to stay with a childhood friend. He was a good kid who attended Catholic school all through elementary and secondary school even though he was not religious at all. We became friends around the third grade and I would spend a good bit of time with him and his family. Mainly, we would play video games and watch movies. I spent many weekends at his house.

As I look back now I do appreciate the love my friend's mother had for the Lord. Anywhere we went she would pray and ask the Lord's blessing to be upon our trip. We would often hear the words "Praise the Lord" as part of her vocabulary. She truly had a sweet and giving spirit. I have not been in contact with the family after enlisting in the Army except for a letter I sent to their house during a deployment in 1997. I did receive a letter from my friend's mother and sister in which I replied. As for my friend he sent no reply.

Shortly after I was saved, I brought my friend to my Uncle's house so that he could share the Gospel with him in the same manner that he shared it with me. My friend was not receptive at all, especially after we made feel that he was less than dirt for not accepting Christ. He has not spoken with me since and I can only pray that he will come to the saving knowledge of the Lord. To this day I am thankful for this family's kindness in taking me in. Regretfully again because of my behavior I was asked to leave. I packed my bags and moved on to my mother and stepfather's home. It was here that I was presented with the solid Gospel for the first time.

Gospel Seed Planted

When I was 16 yrs old, my Uncle (the one I moved in with initially) called me and asked me if I wanted to go fishing. I said sure, on the way to and back from the lake my uncle began to share with me his new found faith in Christ.
He explained to me the need for salvation by putting my faith and trust in Jesus Christ for the forgiveness of sins. He explained to me that I was a sinner.

Romans 3:23 "For all have sinned, and come short of the glory of God."

He explained the penalty for my sin.

Romans 6:23 "For the wages of sin is death; but the gift of God is eternal life through Jesus Christ our Lord."

*He then explained the gift in detail
and what I had to do to receive it.*

Romans 5:8 "But God commendeth his love towards us, in that, while we were yet sinners, Christ died for us."

Romans 10:9-10 "That if thou shall confess with thy mouth the Lord Jesus, and shalt believe in thine heart that God hath raised him from the dead, thou shalt be saved."

After he explained this to me I did say a prayer asking Jesus to save me. However, this was all done in my head and not my heart. Not consciously did I do this but I still did not grasp the heart piece for some reason. The Bible explains this in the parable of the seed (Matthew 13:1-23). I believe verses 20 and 21 are what took place in my situation at that point.

Matthew 13:20-21 But he that received the seed into stony places, the same is he that heareth the word, and anon with joy receiveth it; Yet hath he not root in himself, but dureth for a while: for when tribulation or persecution

ariseth because of the word, by and by he is offended.

After I said the prayer I was excited and went to tell a member of my family about it, thinking she would be just as excited. Her response was that everyone has their own beliefs and that I should not try to push it on her. I then went to tell another family member, he said that I needed to be careful with getting involved with this religion and that my Uncle was just going through some hard times and that it would be months before he was done with it. I was extremely bothered by these responses, not to mention one of my family members saw me shortly after and made a crack at me by asking me if I was going to be a Jesus freak. All this reaction caused me to toss aside my initial joy as these verses state. This religious experience was filed way in a closet for the next two years. I can not remember the topic of religion occurring after this during this time. I went on doing the things teens do without parent supervision which usually ended up in no good.

The independence that I had as a teen caused me to have to be rather defensive which led into fights. Growing up it seemed that a year could not go by without getting into some type of fight. I could not tell you what all of them were about. Some were about girls, others were about respect. I guess that is one of the reasons I am big on respect to this day. I have grown to embrace the philosophy that everyone deserves respect, even the underdogs. I have always had a heart for the underdog and still do to this day. The childhood friend that I lived with was an underdog, but he was my friend and I would defend him when others would try to make fun of him.

I found myself hanging around a few of these underdogs along the way and they sure did keep me out of trouble. As a matter of fact, I would even later marry one.

D-Day

At this point I was 17 years old and had my own apartment after residing with various households from the age of 14. A couple of doors down from my apartment resided a woman who needed help moving an appliance. While I was assisting her I noticed that she was very depressed. I asked her if she was ok and she said that she admitted that her depression was a result of the recent death of her fiance. At this point I had absolutely no idea what to say except, "I am sorry to hear that, from what I see the end of the world may be soon anyways according to Nostradamus". As awkward of a response that sounds she responded well making me feel a little more at ease. She said, "I do not not know all about that, I am going to church now which has been a huge help." She then picked up and handed me a book called 1994 by Harold Camping.[2]

Ironically, Harold Camping made headline news in 2011 with yet another prediction for the end of the world. Back in 1993 he made the same prediction however it was to occur in the fall of 1994. Well as a 17 year old kid I began to have thoughts about not making it to my 18th birthday and began to think about what would happen to me if I were to die in the near future or if the world would end as Mr. Camping was predicting. As I was sorting through all of this thought process

---

[2] Camping, Harold. 1994? Vantage Press, 1992.

and flipping through the pages of this book I did not go back in my mind to the profession of faith in Christ I had made a couple of years prior to this new thought processing of life after death. I also had zero knowledge pertaining to what the Bible states about end time date setting at the time.

Matthew 24:36 But of that day and hour knoweth no man, no, not the angels of heaven, but my Father only.

Later in the year in October of 1993 was a pivotal time in my life due to the fact that I moved once again out of my apartment and I broke up with the girl I thought I was going to marry. On the exact day this break occurred, my uncle not knowing where I was because I had moved around so often was praying for me and felt that he needed to give me a call to see how I was doing. The first place he called was my new residence which happened to be the basement of my mother and stepfather's basement that I rented. When I answered the phone he asked me how I was doing and I explained to him the situation I was in.

He began to preach to me by saying that he was not going to beat around the bush and that Jesus was the only way to salvation. I began to ask all kinds of questions about different religions, dinosaurs, etc. He answered them from the Bible to the point where I could not argue with him. After the conversation, he asked me if I wanted to attend church with him on October 31, 1993 and I agreed.

After the service the preacher asked while we were praying if those that would like prayer for themselves if they did not know where they were going when they died. I raised my hand because I knew I could use all the prayers that I could get. He then asked after the hands were raised if those that raised their hands would like to come forward so someone could show them from the Bible how to be saved. I had no intentions of going forward mainly because I was shy. An old man came up to me and said you already went half way I will walk up with you. So I did. Again, I said a prayer with the altar worker. But really it was that night that I got alone with God and fully submitted my faith, trust, and life to Jesus Christ.

I told God if I was going to be a Christian I wanted to do it right and that if He had the power to save me I believed He could help me overcome my sin. That night I was genuinely saved. The seed had sprung forth from the good soil, and my life had changed from that point on. I became a child of God, spiritually born as spoke about in the book of John.

John 3:3   Jesus answered and said unto him,
Verily, verily, I say unto thee, Except a man be born again,
he cannot see the kingdom of God.

Based on the decision I made that day the portals of Heaven did not visually open before my eyes. I did not hear the angels rejoicing in Heaven. However, I did know that the spiritual transaction was finished. God had redeemed His purchase of my soul and I was now a bonafide child of His that would never be the same. As a result of this glorious change in my life I knew that my behavior would be different. I knew that my friends would no longer be the same. As a matter of fact I had a pager at the time that I turned off. I no longer wanted the temptation to hang out with the party crowd I associated with during most of my teenage years.

Within the next week or so I decided to send letters to family members, teachers, and co-workers about my decision to trust in Christ. I did not expect any response and no response I received. I wanted everyone to know, I even called a former girlfriend who know doubt thought I fell off my rocker. I was hoping that they would embrace the Lord, because in my heart I immediately wanted to have a companion by my side who felt the same way I did and have the same goals. This would come a little later.

HURRY UP AND WAIT

Proverbs 3:5-6 Trust in the LORD with all thine heart;
and lean not unto thine own understanding.
In all thy ways acknowledge him,
and he shall direct thy paths.

Not long at all after my salvation the Lord began to
resurrect previous desires and plans to join the Army. So the
blown off response I received from the novice soldiers earlier
in High School did not deter me from my eventual goal of
becoming a soldier in the United States Army after all. When I
was 17 years old I applied for enlistment at the end of my
senior year of high school. I was pumped to the max when I
got to Military Entrance Processing Station (MEPS) to take my
Armed Forces Aptitude Battery Test and Physical (ASVAB). I
passed my ASVAB with flying colors so all that was left was
the physical.

During the physical the doctor asked me various medical
questions as he went over my medical questionnaire and all of
a sudden he looked at my thumb and noticed the big wart that
was on it. My enlistment processing went downhill when he
began to state that he was not going to qualify me for
enlistment into the Army until I had the wart removed and it
was completely healed. I was crushed and angry to say the
least. How could I be disqualified because of a wart?! He said
that because of its location and size it had the possibility of
getting a cut and infected and the best thing was for the wart

to be removed before enlisting.

I decided to put my plans on the back burner for awhile for a girl I thought I was going to marry and the fact I had no clue how I was going to go about getting the wart removed. Timing is everything and God's timing is perfect. He knew that I had an appointment with redemption and this is why my enlistment was put on hold. I was trying to "hurry up" and God was wanting me to "wait." All it took to put me on hold was a simple wart. There is a plan and purpose even for the ugly and annoying warts in our lives.

Ecclesiastes 3:1 He hath made every thing beautiful in his time: also he hath set the world in their heart, so that no man can find out the work that God maketh from the beginning to the end.

About a year went on and I was working a job breaking down brake calipers in what we called "the pit." I was making $6.50 an hour and came home daily black with brake fluid and dust. What made the matter worse was that I did not have a shower, only a bathtub. So you can imagine what my tub water might have looked like. It was time for a change and I felt led to call my recruiters after I was able to successfully have the wart laser removed with the insurance I had at the caliper shop. Of course they were glad to hear from me, I was a "Grad A," which is someone who is in the top tier educationally for enlistment. The funny part is that years later while serving as a recruiter I ran into one of the recruiters who worked at the recruiting station who remembered my name on the dry erase board. The recruiters did their job well getting me through the enlistment process and they one of the first few recruits I would attempt to enlist in the LORD's Army by inviting them to church.

As for the reaction of the church, when I began to share with others about my decision to join the Army, I did not get the reaction I would have hoped to. Some Christians acted as if I was joining Satan's army by their reactions. In other words, they felt that as a new Christian I would not survive as a believer if I was not in a church structured environment. They felt the only safe place was in their religious bubble. Sometimes, I wonder if these people fail to realize that God does not live in a man's religious bubble.

Isaiah 55:8-9 For my thoughts are not your thoughts,
neither are your ways my ways, saith the LORD.
For as the heavens are higher than the earth,
so are my ways higher than your ways,
and my thoughts than your thoughts.

Many years later I would learn what these religious bubbles or in friendlier terms "church structured environment" would mean. Much has to do with power, control, and commercialism. There is no doubt in my mind that many Christian leaders know that there is liberty in Christ; but for whatever reason, most likely due to fear, they do all they can to keep "their" sheep within the confines of "their" pens.

The irony of it all is that I received this type of negative reaction from those who I thought would rejoice with for just about everything that God has called me to do. At the time I was not ready to understand this type of rejection because it was a time of bottle fed growth. I was just a newborn Christian trusting in my older brothers and sisters to care for me pending my ship off date to Basic Training. However, now I understand very well that it all boils down to, and that is love. The unconditional love of my father or mother for instance says, "Do what you are meant to do son, we support you" regardless if it means a sacrifice on our part. Those who lack love say, "Do what is best for our interest, organization, and cause...we are not willing to make such sacrifices."

So, I was hurried through the enlistment process in January of 1994 and now it was time to wait.

As a new believer I became a sponge taking in all that I could. I began to attend a college and career Sunday School class at a local Independent Fundamental Baptist (IFB) church. This is the same church that my uncle who led me to the LORD attends even unto this day. My initial thought was that everyone that parked their car in his church parking lot and sat in one of the pews was on fire for Jesus. I quickly learned that this was not the case at all. I also thought that now that I was saved sinful thoughts would no longer formulate in my mind.

As for the bad thoughts I did not know a whole lot of hymns or spiritual music. I didn't even know that the Bible spoke about casting down imaginations and singing to ourselves spiritual songs and hymns. Somehow that is exactly what I did, the only downside was that my spiritual music selection was very slim to none. So I would be singing songs like Silent Night and it was nowhere near Christmas.

2 Corinthians 10:5   Casting down imaginations, and every high thing that exalteth itself against the knowledge of God, and bringing into captivity every thought to the obedience of Christ;

When it came to the "not so on fire for Jesus" folks all I could think of is that I hoped that they would come to the same understanding of who the Lord is and experience the joy that had been bestowed upon me then and still burns in my heart until this day.

One day my uncle and I returned from a nursing home where we were able to share the Gospel to a group of elderly folks. That day professions of faith were made and we walked away excited not being able to wait to tell our church mates. I shared the news as a testimony in the college and career Sunday School class. Towards the end of the class there was a group of young adults that had grown up in the church and I thought to myself that they would like to hear more details about our nursing home experience that day.

I approached the group and began to share the details of our nursing home visit. The group got rather quiet and there was a moment of silence. I then received a look of "O.K???..." and they resumed their conversation about the movies they saw over the weekend. I began to understand very quickly that just because a person went to church it did not mean you were on fire for the Lord.

A Soldier's Progress

2 Timothy 3:5   Having a form of godliness,
but denying the power thereof: from such turn away.

Even so, there were those who were on fire for the Lord and these are the people I learned the most from. For instance, there was an elderly man around eighty years old who was a greeter and held the door open as people filed into the sanctuary. I noticed one Sunday morning that he has tears running down his face. I asked my uncle later why he was crying and he told me that he was saved later in life. He was so grateful that the Lord got a hold of his heart before he was snatched from this world that he could not help but cry. His tears spoke volumes.

Godly elderly saints have a vital and significant role in the church. They often may feel as if they do not have much to offer, but in reality it has been these saints who have had a huge impact on my spiritual development. We must never forget that "Little is Much When God Is in It"[3], even a single tear that runs down a man or woman's face. This would not be the first time either that I would be impacted by genuine ministry from an elderly saint.

Little is Much When God Is in It Refrain:
Little is much when God is in it,
Labor not for wealth or fame;
There's a crown, and you can win it,
If you go in Jesus' name.

---

[3] Suffield, Kittie L. Hymn, 1924.

I drew much strength from these early positive experiences with God's people. I do not remember too many negative experiences at all. It seemed that many that I came in contact with were glad to see this mullet sporting teen give his life to the Lord. I suppose they could see the genuine conversion in my life which caused them to praise the Lord and be encouraged in their own walks.

Speaking of the mullet, that would soon be gone. As I said when I called upon the Lord for salvation, I want to please the Lord in every area of life. One of the areas that I was convicted of early on was my hair. It may or may not have been more of a symbolic gesture of the change that was wrought in my life. Nevertheless, the Scripture that states it is a shame for a man to have long hair was enough for me. The good thing is I do not have to worry about long hair anymore, except for the long beard I am currently working on, because I have no longer have much hair on head.

The timing on my hair was perfect because in November the following month after my salvation I was baptized. This truly was a great day! I was so thankful and glad to be able to tell the whole church I was now a child of God and that my life would never be the same. The assistant pastor at the time baptized me at my request. I requested this pastor because I felt that he was the underdog who served with a senior/founding pastor who had great charisma in his preaching style. I liked the senior pastor's boldness and lack of fear concerning what others thought of him. I could tell the assistant was a little intimidated by this and I thought I would encourage him by asking if he would baptize me. After I enlisted in the Army I periodically sent the assistant pastor who is now the senior pastor a note to let him know how I was doing. He would always respond with a kind note in return even though he has never recognized the ministry of The Soldier's Sanctuary.

Matthew 28:19   Go ye therefore, and teach all nations, baptizing them in the name of the Father, and of the Son, and of the Holy Ghost:

During this time of waiting to ship off to Basic Training I moved in with my aunt and uncle which was beneficial for me financially and spiritually. My uncle took the time to disciple me using a 12 lesson discipleship series. I carefully and with much thought read through each lesson and remember getting my uncle excited by challenging him with questions concerning areas I did not understand. At the same time, I would share with him the golden treasures I was discovering for the first time while reading and studying the Bible.

2 Timothy 2:15   Study to shew thyself approved unto God, a workman that needeth not to be ashamed, rightly dividing the word of truth.

My growth continued as I studied and meditated on the Word of God. There was something also growing in my heart during these newborn days and time of waiting to ship off to Basic Training. The need for a companion in my life was once again surfacing. This has always been a need in my life since I was a little boy. I have had a strong attraction to women ever since I could remember. I even has a crush on my first grade teacher. This time I wanted someone who loved the Lord as I loved the Lord.

On Valentine's day there was a girl I met while assisting with a bus route that picked up kids to go to church. She was very outgoing and seemed very sincere in her service for God. There was only one problem, I have always been rather shy and had to work up to my initial approach. So I decided to send her a Valentine's card to no avail.

I am not sure but I think that her Dad may have put the brakes on that attempt because he did not think that I had the package that was good enough for his daughter. He probably could not get the mullet I sported out of his head, nor the fact that I was not college bound at the time, but Army bound. I know now it just was not meant to be and that the Lord had someone else that He had planned for me whom I love very much. This memoir will go into great detail on how I met that exact person that God intended me to spend the rest of my life with.

Proverbs 18:22   Whoso findeth a wife findeth
a good thing, and obtaineth favour of the LORD.

It was not a long time between my ship date and the day of my salvation. However, I feel that it was a great time of growth, reflection, spiritual campaigns, and preparation for what was to come in the future. Little did I know that I would soon be off the spiritual baby formula and would be drinking milk on my own. The spiritual campaigns and exercises that were conducted while serving at this initial church proved to be rather beneficial even unto this day. I learned to be bold for my newfound faith as bold as the senior pastor I respected. There were so many opportunities and I wanted to be part of every effort that I could in the short amount of time that I had left before I left for the Army. Each opportunity proved to be greatly formative and productive which I am thankful for.

I was on a mission for the glory of God, I wanted the world to know that the new Andy was alive. One day I was at a local store and I ran into someone from high school who was not very popular at all. We knew of each other but we did not "know" each other. I gave him a Gospel tract which he immediately looked at and then looked at me and said "yeah right!" laughed and then walked away. He thought it was a joke. There is no doubt it would have to be much time before people that knew of me were going to be impacted by the testimony of the "new" Andy that was for sure. In a way it made perfect sense to receive my orders from the Lord to ship off to the Army. Nevertheless, I did my best to reach out to all those I came in contact with throughout my life.

I had an ex-girlfriend (fiance) that was a priority spiritual target for me and I was hoping that she would embrace the Lord as I did. She simply stated that she was not ready for the type of change I was hoping for. I knew in the back of my mind that there was no hope of rekindling the relationship. Even though I was tempted to dampen my zeal in order to try to win her back, I did not. I am glad God protected me from certain misery that would have occurred if I were to marry outside of His will.

My parents and family once again became priority targets
for witnessing as well. I wrote them a letter detailing my
conversion. I even sought reconciliation with my step mother
because of our broken relationship growing up. Again I did
not get the response that I hoped for. They did express their
appreciation for my thoughtfulness and concern. Whether
they agreed with me or not I do feel that deep inside each of
them knew the recent change in my life was for the good.

I continued to reach out to the previous contacts I had made
in my life. I even sent my high school auto tech teacher a note.
I made it through his class by the skin of my teeth and by his
grace because he could have easily failed me due to my
attendance and participation. I wanted him to know that I had
embraced a new responsibility in my life and made a great
step of faith. I am sure he received the letter because it was not
returned. This attempt and others would receive no response.
The sad reality of the lack of response is that I initially thought
that many would commend me for this noble decision I made
in my life. Instead it seemed to be the opposite. People were
perfectly content with my previous destructive lifestyle as
long as I did not hurt them or anyone else. Now taking a stand
for the Lord was different! Oh poor Andy...he has went off the
deep end, I hope he recovers soon. Well, I suppose I have
never recovered to their standard and by the grace of God I
never will.

I sure did enjoy reaching out to others as I still do. I feel that
I am on a constant mission for the glory of God. I remember
one door that I knocked on with my Uncle, I did not know
much but I did know my testimony of how I accepted the Lord
in my life. I shared my story with this woman and was

touched by the tears that came to her eyes. The power of God was with us and spoke to her heart that day. I knew that I wanted to be used of God to reach people in this manner for the rest of my life.

I am not sure this motive is what drives others to reach out to others in the same manner. One day I drove to Columbus, Ohio area to help out a new church plant. I went with a man who seemed to be zealous for the Lord. We talked all the way to our start point until we finally arrived and he introduced me to one of my favorite preachers of all time- Lester Roloff. This was a preacher who loved the Lord and did not care what others thought of him. He preached a message entitled "The Mule Walked On" and even to this day I still use the line "and the mule walked on."

Our mission that day was to go door knocking at the dormitories on the college campus. We knocked on a particular door and my partner was the initial speaker and he kept on insisting that we come into his dormitory before he would continue the conversation. The student kindly refused and my partner annoyingly kept on insisting. Finally, I just stepped in and began to share my testimony with him and asked him if there was a time in his life that he had done similar. He sincerely responded, "No, I have not". I then began to lead the man to the Lord and pray with him.

We walked away from the dormitory and I was prepared to rejoice with my partner. However he was not in the rejoicing mood. As a matter of fact his reply was "Alright, you got that one". I immediately told him I did not get nothing and that the Lord is the one who did the work. I hope what I said sunk in. The sad reality is there are countless "Christians" working to put feathers in their caps instead of putting crowns before the Lord's feet, all so they can rise on the social ladder of churchdom. Well, they can keep that ladder because it is an extremely dangerous one that always ends up with a hard fall.

Even though these types of occurrences have irritated me over the years I have not allowed them to distract me. Besides the reality is that each of us must continually be on guard concerning our motives and why we do what we do. Are we attempting to please our denomination or church leadership? Or are we setting out to please the LORD? As I look back, I can not help but to see the chains of organizational worship. In other words the people worship their denominational title more than the God they claim to serve. These leaders surround themselves with loyal and like minded people. The sad reality is that many of these same people are not very loyal anyways and end up burning their leaders in one way or another.

As a brand new Christian I only saw the positive side for the most part and would not want to have had to process the dark side of the ministry. I did not fully understand the negativity until later as pieces were added to the puzzle of my faith. It seems like everyday a piece is added and I see the picture clearer and clearer everyday. I treasure very much the positive memories from all those who genuinely had a heart for the Lord and was willing to take the time to a direct or indirect influence on a babe in Christ.

These memories and lessons were packed along with my packing list for Basic Training where more memories and lessons would be created. The time of learning and discipleship that I received from my uncle during this "Hurry Up and Wait" period was crucial in my life and sustained me in the absence of spiritual mentorship from other men. Thank God for those who allow themselves to be used selflessly for the spiritual development of others.

2 Timothy 2:2   And the things that thou hast heard of me among many witnesses, the same commit thou to faithful men, who shall be able to teach others also.

BASIC TRAINING

The anticipation had now ceased, I was finally on a new leg of my journey and on a plane for the first time in my life. Carefully placed in my pocket was the Gideon Bible I received at the Military Entrance Processing Station. I would open that Bible throughout my training and it brought me much peace and comfort. I really enjoy the description, from an unknown suspected 19th century author[4], the Gideon's put in the front pages of their published New Testaments with Psalms and Proverbs they distribute throughout the world.

"THE BIBLE contains the mind of God, the state of man, the way of salvation, the doom of sinners, and the happiness of believers. Its doctrines are holy, its precepts are binding, its histories are true, and its decisions are immutable. Read it to be wise, believe it to be safe, and practice it to be holy. It contains light to direct you, food to support you, and comfort to cheer you.

It is the traveler's map, the pilgrim's staff, the pilot's compass, the soldier's sword, and the Christian's charter. Here Paradise is restored, Heaven opened, and the gates of hell disclosed.

CHRIST is its grand subject, our good the design, and the

---

[4] The Gideons International. Blog Comment May 18, 2011.
http://blog.gideons.org/2010/12/the-bible-contains-the-mind-of-god/#comment-599

glory of God its end.

It should fill the memory, rule the heart, and guide the feet. Read it slowly, frequently, and prayerfully. It is a mine of wealth, a paradise of glory, and river of pleasure. It is given you in life, will be opened at the judgment, and be remembered forever. It involves the highest responsibility, will reward the greatest labor, and will condemn all who trifle with its sacred contents:"

Author Unknown

These words which beautifully describe the Word of God have resonated in my mind and heart as much now as it did back then. I took this excerpt very seriously and understood that I was on a mission not only to graduate from my initial entry training, but I also had the awesome responsibility of sharing this profound truth with my fellow soldiers. God granted me the boldness and desire by His Spirit to do exactly that. I did my best to share my newfound faith with all that I came in contact with starting with my roommate at the hotel the night prior to flying out for Basic Training to include the group of future soldiers that boarded the plane with us. I can only wonder where some of these folks are now and if those Gospel encounters are part of their testimonies today.

We never will know how much just a few words will impact a person. I was told a story[5] about a man who gave his life to the Lord and was strongly compelled to go downtown

---

[5] Story of Lawyer's Salvation and the Faithful Witness. Unknown

in Cleveland and post himself on a platform by the terminal
tower. He did not know much about the Bible and as he stood
on the platform he yelled out just one Bible. He proclaimed
this verse over and over and did not expound on anything else
due to his limited knowledge.

*John 3:18 He that believeth on him is not condemned:
but he that believeth not is condemned already, because he
hath not believed in the name of the only begotten Son of
God.*

A lawyer was walking by and heard this man shouting at
the top of his lungs this verse over and over and became
irritated. He finally stopped and asked the man, "Hey! If you
are going to stand up there and speak and message, why don't
you say something more than just that verse!" The lawyer then
walked away with that same verse playing over and over in
his head. When he arrived to his office and sat down to start
his work for the day he could not shake the verse from his
mind. It began to seep down from his mind to his heart and
soul which caused him to weep. He then cried out to the Lord
for salvation and his life was forever changed!

The faithful witness who stood on the platform proclaiming
the little that he knew was used of God to put a fire in another
man's soul. He may never in this lifetime realize the impact
that he had on the lawyer's life because of his faithfulness. I
can only wonder about the same concerning the opportunities
the LORD puts in our paths.

A Soldier's Progress

Luke 16:10 He that is faithful in that which is least is faithful also in much: and he that is unjust in the least is unjust also in much.

I was amazed to see God work mightily within our platoon. Some made professions of faith and others rejected the Lord or held to their religious beliefs. Either way the Gospel was shared with them and the Gospel seeds were planted. For those that were interested I started a Bible study and was glad to see a couple of my fellow soldiers gather around my bunk as we discussed the Lord. I was also able to fellowship with other Christians I was able to identify as we shined our boots. Yes! we used to shine our black boots back then. To keep from getting kiwi on our barracks floor we would meet in our common area between platoons where there was plenty of open floor space. In the early 2000's boot shining would cease due to new uniforms in which boots were a sand colored suede type of boot and not a black leather type.

Throughout my Initial Entry Training I was growing very rapidly as I strove to understand the theology that I had learned up to that point. One way of doing this was to debate various doctrinal interpretations. Not sure it was overall fruitful, but it did cause me to search the Scripture in a deeper manner. Since then I rarely get into these types of arguments, mainly because I am confident and have peace with the understanding that the Lord has given me over the years. Not to mention the fact that my mission is to see people start worshipping the Lord, not analyze, critique, and judge their style of worship. There is an evident purpose for diversity within the church that is based on personalities and for the purpose of keeping us humble. We also have to be careful to allow others to grow.

Romans 14:1   Him that is weak in the faith receive ye, but not to doubtful disputations.

I began to see a little of the diversity that would take me so long to realize was acceptable to a point. I did my best to be an example for that which I was preaching. However, my example at times shined and at other times it was very dim, maybe even flickering. The good news it never burnt out completely and never will! Many of the flickering days I have faced has been related to pride. It took me awhile to learn that respect is a two-way street. Respect has developed into one of my most sacred peeves and I feel, and rightfully so, that everyone has the right to be treated with dignity and respect. So when someone crosses the line of respect I tend to push them back across. Sometimes tactfully and sometimes not, which is one of my weaknesses that I must continually work on.

One day while in Basic Training there was a soldier that responded disrespectfully to something I had said about spiritual matters. My response was not respectful at all and was definitely one of my light flickering days. I put my finger in his face and told him he was nothing but a "fag!" You could feel the silence permeate the room which would not be the only moments of silence I have experienced throughout my journey because of my flesh triggered actions. Satan and his henchman no doubt want to destroy our testimony for the Lord. I am just glad that the Lord always works the bad situation in the end through respectful dialogue which should have occurred right from the beginning.

Mark 12:31 And the second is like, namely this, Thou shalt love thy neighbour as thyself. There is none other commandment greater than these.

Marksmanship

Much of Basic Training consists of rifle range training with the overall training success being determined by the outcome of the unit's marksmanship performance. At the end of Basic Rifle Training each soldier would find themselves behind the iron site of an M16A2 rifle and start picking of each GI Johnny Pop-Up target one by one as they appeared from behind their dirt berms. I wanted our unit to be successful to include my own personal performance ending with an "Expert" rating. So, I decided to step out on faith.

Just prior to leaving for the qualification range I told my platoon that I had prayed and asked God to help every soldier on our platoon pass with at least a "Marksman" rating. This was a huge step of faith because our Drill Sergeants were not aware of any other units accomplishing such a feat prior to my request. We all made it to the range and gave our best during our qualifications. Miraculously! We all passed the first time! I even achieved "Expert!" When we returned to the barracks I was quick to give God the glory and was excited to see a couple more soldiers join our Barracks Bible study afterwards.

Basic Training was absolutely beneficial to my start as a soldier in the United States Army and as a soldier of Jesus Christ. For the first time in my life I was able to meet people from all across the country. Each new person I met help me to see the seemingly endless amount of diversity that exists within God's creation. These early experiences began to shape my understanding of people in general which has greatly benefited me towards God's calling in my life.

The first stop of my Initial Entry Training would soon come to an end. No real horror stories to tell, as a matter of fact, I would later tell my soldiers as an Infantryman that they had 24 hours to tell their basic training stories and if we heard any after that they would get their bags smoked. In other words, go through some very strenuous physical fitness exercises to jar their memories. Basic had its physical and mental challenges; however it was very doable, especially with the Lord at your side.

VICTORY

I graduated from Army Basic Training in May of 1994. No
one attended my graduation so I ended up spending our
family day with other families. When our graduation was
completed we were loaded on buses and headed for Fort
Gordon, Georgia where I would begin my job training (AIT) in
the communications job I selected when I first enlisted. I was
definitely looking for more freedom when we arrived at Fort
Gordon. The first couple of weeks were basically in lock-down
mode, but after that we were free to enjoy life after training
and on the weekends. Free, as long as we did not get into any
trouble. Sadly, it was not long before I found myself in trouble.

There was a soldier in my class who was short and of
Mexican descent who was rather calm in nature. One fine day
in our class break room we happened to be debating about
biblical matters. Something was said that by this soldier fired
up. Next thing I know I was standing right in front of him
with my finger in is face and said, "what are you going to do
about it!" Then, WHAM, he punched me right in my nose. I
was irate! It took the whole class to stop me from wringing
this kids neck. The situation was brought under control by our
soldier classmates and the instructor as they pulled us apart.
There was blood streaming from my nose so our instructor
sent me immediately to the hospital.

When I arrived at the hospital I found out that my nose was
broken. I could not believe my nose was broken. Feelings were
brewing inside and I knew the only thing that I could do was
pray. I began to pray and ask the Lord for strength to do the

right thing. I said, "Lord, I am going to do one of two things. I am either going to go back and wring that kids neck, or you are going to have to give me the strength to apologize for creating the hostile situation that I did." Needless to say, the Lord gave me the strength to apologize to this soldier for my actions. After I apologized he told me that he did not know what overcame him. He said he had never hit anyone like that in his life and thought I was going to kill him. I told him that I knew who allowed him to do what he did and I explained to him that it was God and that I deserved it. I am glad I responded by owning up to my actions, in doing so, my momentary foe decided to become my friend and attend church with me.

Ephesians 4:31-32   Let all bitterness, and wrath, and anger, and clamour, and evil speaking, be put away from you, with all malice: And be ye kind one to another, tenderhearted, forgiving one another, even as God for Christ's sake hath forgiven you.

When I was in my job training at Ft. Gordon I was seeking to attend an Independent Baptist Church (IFB.) The Lord lead me to do some research so I began to call a couple of churches. I got a hold of one particular church by the name of Victory Baptist Church in North Augusta, SC. I began to question the man about where the church stood and I remember most definitely asking whether or not the church took a stand for the King James Version. The man said that they did and began to inform me that they had a church bus that picked up soldiers from the base. The next Sunday the bus came and I arrived for my first visit with a church who loves soldiers and was thoughtful enough to reach out to us.

I was there for a few weeks and was enjoying the services very much. While I was attending I was looking for a solid Christian girl to meet. There were two that stood out to me, one was my wife the other was another pretty girl that was in my Sunday school class and who I also saw at a singles ministry gathering. There was a big difference that caught my attention between these two young women. My wife sat in front of the church and I could tell she loved the Lord just by her reaction to the worship service. The other seemed to want to drift away from spiritual conversation which disturbed me very much. This was all a learning process for me, because I thought that everyone that parked their car in the church parking lot and sat down in the pew loved the Lord. I began to find out this was not the case. I began to wonder if I would find anyone anytime soon who had the passion for the things of God as he had planted in my heart.

Lin, my wife, would come and shake the soldier's hands each week. She felt it was a ministry and was burdened to do so especially after a blessing she received from a soldier's family. Lin wanted to be a blessing to the visiting soldiers, so she took the time to make Christmas cards for the soldiers. One of the soldiers later died and as the wife was going through her husband's belongings she came upon one of Lin's Christmas cards. The card touched her so much she gave 10% from the insurance money that she had received and gave it to my wife's church along with a testimony of the blessing. It is because of this my wife felt led to continue to minister to the soldiers who came to her church with this type of continued kind gestures.

I am glad the Lord led Lin to be friendly to us because I was shy and it would have been very difficult for me to approach her on my own. One Sunday I worked up enough nerve to ask her how she was doing and I noticed she had work clothes on so I asked her where she worked at. I still was not used to the southern dialect of the south and I thought she said she worked at Wendy's which I was very familiar with. The next day I called Wendy's from the barracks and asked for Linda Fielding. The woman who answered the phone stated that she was not in and asked if she could take a message. I said sure and relayed the message along with my phone number.

A couple of days went by and no response. I decided to try once again, and I received the same response. After this I felt like a stalker. Here lies my mistake, I should have prayed. Instead of praying I began to make excuses why I should not go back to Lin's church. I said to myself, "because I have shown those people my passion for what I believe, they have now just brushed me aside to look for more numbers." Plus, I did not want to face Lin because I thought she might be thinking that I was stalking her. I let negative thoughts control and direct me instead of seeking the Lord's guidance. During these few weeks that I did not attend Lin's church I attended the chapel on post, but it was not the same. I made some wrong decisions to consume alcohol and even found myself at a strip club one evening. However, I could not escape the Lord and his conviction.

A Soldier's Progress

*Luke 15:4   What man of you, having an hundred sheep,
if he lose one of them, doth not leave the ninety and nine in
the wilderness, and go after that which is lost, until he find
it?*

As I was drinking a beer in a bar late one night, I ended up witnessing to a girl that I met while there. I was definitely under the influence and decided to go outside where I told the five or six soldiers I was with that I was a Christian. I told them that might choose to attend the bark and drink that night was foolish and I asked them if I could huddle up with them up for a word of prayer. I do not remember the exact words that I prayed, I am just amazed the soldiers were willing to pray with me and did not just walk away.

Later that night we were stopped by the MP's while going through the gate on the way back to the barracks and I was questioned as to whether or not I had been drinking. I said no. I was then released to my unit where I had to write a statement. In the statement I wrote that I was a Christian and that I should have not been doing what I was doing. I wrote that I had lied to the MP's and that whatever punishment I should receive I deserved. No punishment ever came, I suppose my superiors felt that I was punished enough.

*Proverbs 20:1   Wine is a mocker, strong drink is raging:
and whosoever is deceived thereby is not wise.*

Not long after my bar episode, a few soldiers and I planned to go roller skating. When we arrived at the roller rink it was closed. So, low and behold, there was a strip club right across the street. My comrades decided that they wanted to go to the strip club. I began to justify to myself that I could play pool while I waited for them so we could split the cab fare back. Well, it obviously did not work out that way. As the stripper came out I felt utterly ashamed. I was so ashamed that I put my head down and acted like I was asleep. There was a man that was a couple of rows ahead of me who decided he was going to be funny and throw a cigarette butt at me. I did not take to kindly to this jester and went off him by telling him, "let's step outside right now so I can beat you down." He asked me, "are you drunk?" I told him that I hadn't drank anything and that I was a Christian and should not be in that type of place. This man and the stripper looked at me as though if I was crazy and nothing more was said.

After these two major instances I decided that I was fed up with all of this and that I was going back to Victory Baptist Church so that I could stay on the right path regardless if Lin thought I was a stalker or not. I was going back for God and nobody else! The first Sunday that I arrived back to Victory, during hand shaking time, Lin approached me and asked me, "where have you been?" I told her it was along story and that I was glad to be back. I figured since I had her there, I told her about my attempts to call her at Wendy's. She said, "Wendy's! I work at Winn-Dixie!" I thought to myself "Winn-Dixie!" you have got to be kidding me! All this time because of that wonderful southern accent I thought she said Wendy's. After my shock cleared I asked Lin for her number and she gave it to me.

I called Lin that evening and we talked a good while about

our testimonies and love for the Lord. I did not know this at the time but after our conversation my wife talked to her Dad (Larry) who was away at a job as a union welder. She told him, "Dad, I met the man I am going to marry!" It was three weeks later on my birthday I felt led of the Lord to propose to Lin. The amazing part about it is that Lin prayed as a little girl to be proposed to on a rock that was back behind her house in the woods next to a stream, which I did not know. Guess where I proposed to her, on the rock. I took my Bible with us as we went to that rock, I had a ring tied to the divider string in the bible, I had marked and highlighted Psalms 118:23 with "Will You Marry Me" on the bottom of the page. She said, "YES!!!!!!!!!!!" And, I still have this Bible today.

Psalms 118:23 This is the LORD'S doing;
it is marvellous in our eyes.

I said all of this to say trust God and pray. It is too easy to make excuses and to justify our sin. I am glad the Lord had taught me these lessons very early in my Christian walk because I needed to go on to learn bigger and greater things, especially in the realm of religion which can be more dangerous than any alcoholic beverage or strip club.

BATTLE BUDDY

June 23, 1995 was our big wedding day. No doubt we were both looking forward to this life changing day we would both experience. The LORD perfectly orchestrated all of the events that led to our sacred union. It is what I had prayed for and believed that God wanted for the both of us. Since the day of my salvation it was my desire to meet a woman after his own heart. God not only answered the prayer but he had the preacher who married us confirm it on our wedding day. Just before the ceremony, he told me, "Son, you could not have picked a better girl in our entire church." The preacher was and is absolutely correct, there could be no better girl waiting for me because Lin is the girl that God had always intended for me.

My wife is my spiritual battle buddy on this road called life. Without her companionship I would have made it as far as we have traveled together. We have learned from each other and continue to challenge each other in our spiritual growth and walk with the Lord. I am very much thankful for her Christian upbringing and the steadfast she has learned from her parents. Lin's father was a union welder who gave his life to the Lord in his mid-twenties and married at the age of 27. The first time I met him was at the church we were all attending at the time and I must say he looked a little intimidating. He surely did not look like your run of the mill suited up IFB church member. He had on jeans, an untucked dress shirt, and a scraggly beard. I was a little nervous to meet him considering this was the first time I ever met him face to face and already had asked his daughter to marry me.

I would soon learn that Larry Fielding was a humble man who had a genuine love for the Lord. You could also see that it was obvious that he did not care what anyone thought concerning his faith and how he walked with the Lord to include his church brethren. From what I saw from others Larry was highly respected and I respected him just the same for the short time I was able to fellowship with him before his death. The determination, devotion, and steadfastness that Larry possessed was inherited by his daughter which is still evident today as it was when she was growing up. I was amazed at how much my wife and her siblings revered their Dad. Each of them joyously mentioned that their father was faithful to read his Bible daily even if it was a few verses so that he could research and meditate on the short passage more thoroughly. I was very much impacted by this man's devotion to the Lord.

One day I arrived to my wife's house before noon. Lin did tell me that her dad stated that arriving before noon was not a good idea due to their schedule. Come to find out, this schedule involved Larry's prayer time. When I arrived to the house I saw Larry walking in the woods behind their house. He had a Bible in one hand and some coffee in the other. You could see him audibly speaking with the Lord. This live footage was true spirituality in action which was priceless for me to witness.

This steadfast dedicated character is just one of the few traits that my spiritual battle buddy and help meet would adopt. The best part of it all is that she was able to even maintain her love and devotion for the Lord in the midst of persecution at her own church and "Christian" school while growing up. As we look back now we know that these trials are no doubt a part of God's spiritual development plan for our lives and if they are accepted in this light we can praise God for molding and shaping us in the vessel that he would have us to be.

John 15:19-20 If ye were of the world, the world would love his own: but because ye are not of the world, but I have chosen you out of the world, therefore the world hateth you. Remember the word that I said unto you, The servant is not greater than his lord. If they have persecuted me, they will also persecute you; if they have kept my saying, they will keep yours also.

One of the issues that Lin faced was that she inherited a hair gene from her father. This hair gene caused her to have more hair on her arms then normal which her parents at first did not allow to be shaven off. This caused her great grief because her fellow students starting calling her "ALF" (from the television series) and "Lin-dog." Throughout this ridicule and other episodes she maintained her love, passion, and devotion for the Lord. Ironically, the "Christian" students even found her steadfastness for the Lord to be a topic of ridicule.

I am still amazed today at how people are deceived to believe that the "Christian" schools are the only acceptable means of education. I myself remember walking by a Christian school on my way to an inner city public Middle School, which I would not now send one of my dogs to, and thought to myself "Man! These kids are worse than the city kids I have to put up with everyday!" Lin's experience and mine together would no doubt impact and influence our educational decisions for our children later down the road. God has laid out a specific path for us that was not dictated by any man. We have refused to bow down to the church coercion that has been blasted from the pulpit with the effort to manipulate their congregations into supporting their substandard and hypocritical modes of education in the guise of teaching our kids the Bible.

This is just one of the stands that Lin and I would have to face on our spiritual journey together. Education would not be the only decision we would have to take a stand against the puppet masters. I never thought we would end up one day fighting against a corrupt religious system while doing our best to reach the lost. All I know is that I could not have received a better spiritual battle buddy than my beautiful wife to fight by my side. No wonder the battle buddy principle is practiced in our military. As a Drill Sergeant I have enforced this principle over and over. The enemy is always seeking to destroy us, so having more than one set of eyes looking out for us is always a plus.

God has richly blessed us with four wonderful children-Judah, Jesse, Jacquelin, and Larry. I am sure you may have noticed three "J" names and then saw "Larry." Many have said or thought, "What?" I am sure you understand from the mention of my father-in-law which I will explain in more detail later on why we name our youngest son after him. Larry does have a "J" in his name though. His middle name is Justice which is an alternate spelling to Justus in the Bible. I really like how he is referred to. Our battle buddy team of Lin and I has now turned into a fire team and basically a squad if you include our animals.

Humanly speaking, I can take only a small portion of the credit pertaining to the overall bind that God has blessed our family with. If we had to give anyone credit other than God, who gets all the credit, it would be my wife. She has devoted all of her time and energy into our children with a sacrificial love. She has not only devoted her being to God and her family, she has showed the same sacrificial love towards others without thought of return. Any good that I have been able to contribute to our household is just from doing my best to apply what I have learned in the Bible and seen others practice in their own families. However, I have failed many times. Just ask my wife and kids.

Our de facto missionary family to the military fulfilled my wife's calling that she received as a little girl. She never dreamed this calling would be fulfilled by marrying a soldier and later serving in a ministry called The Soldier's Sanctuary. The greatest part God orchestrated his mission for us in the most unconventional way, after all we do serve an unconventional God. In other words, you or I can not put him in a box. God created the puzzle pieces of our journey and put them together in his timing. He did reveal a piece here and there along the way while he was leading us; however, the picture was not clear until we actually crossed the line of obedience. Lin and I have been able to reflect over the past years and can see now exactly why certain instances have occurred in each of lives to bring us where we are at today.

My beautiful missionary wife has been a huge and internal

part of our ministry starting from our church plant, previous ministry work, and where we are at today. As I am writing now we are yet on another missionary journey meeting new people and making new connections for the glory of God. Lin's outgoing and joyful spirit has greatly impacted our outreach. She has a way of making people smile and feel good about life. She has absolutely no problem sharing the Gospel either. She truly looks for every opportunity to share her faith. I am forever grateful and thankful to have her as my Battle Buddy!

DOGFACE SOLDIER

As newlyweds, my wife and I had a short stay not to far where she grew up. I had temporary orders at Fort Gordon for some additional training I was taking for my communications job while assigned to a Signal Battalion at Fort Stewart, Georgia which is now known as the 3rd Infantry Division. We lived in a run down trailer in a small trailer park and drove a three cylinder Geo Metro. It made no difference to us because we had been love struck and it was our home. The trailer park was also right across the street from where our local church at the time held their annual sawdust tent meeting. This same tent meeting location was the same spot I surrender to God's calling upon my life.

Not sure what night of the week it was, but I decided to go forward and make it known that the Lord had called me to preach his Holy Word to a lost and dying world. I was so nervous I was practically shaking while I approached the first man I recognized at the altar. His family happened to live in the same trailer park that we did. At the point of my declaration, the man knew what to do and began to pray. I do not remember the words, but do appreciate him taking the time to do so. Within the same week or so, I wanted my words to be action and I began preaching at the local county jail with wife's Dad which was a huge honor to me. I admired and appreciated his unpolished preaching style that was straight from the heart.

One Sunday we went into a cell block together and I was in awe as I listened to the words flow out of Larry's mouth and heart. He would bounce around from one thing to the next. He would say "God made the flowers and he made the bees to pollinate the flowers…" I am paraphrasing, because you would have to be there to hear the word pictures he was painting that transitioned into a salvation message. He was simply allowing the Lord to use him as a paint brush. After that day I was determined if I was going to preach God's Word I wanted to be used in the same manner. I must say that I was beyond nervous as I preached at that jail. However, God always delivered the boldness when it was needed as he still does today. Those nerves that God allowed me to experience were no doubt a huge window for the purpose of displaying the passion that he has given me for the mission that I am called too.

Acts 4:13 Now when they saw the boldness of Peter and John, and perceived that they were unlearned and ignorant men, they marvelled; and they took knowledge of them, that they had been with Jesus.

As God was working in our lives at that small trailer park, the devil was working also. Those first few months of our marriage were exciting, yet rough. Lin had high expectations and I had a lot of baggage from the old man which consisted mainly of selfishness. I have gotten better over the years but it is still something that I battle with daily and that I have to work at. Many of our early issues had to do with where I was spending my time. Much of my time involved the Army which had left me drained and often does still to this day. The other time zapper would have to be the computer in some way, fashion, or form. So, I would end up allowing myself to be spent by these two activities which would lead to heated arguments. The irony is that I spent more time arguing and could have satisfied by wife's need for fellowship in half of the time.

As we slowly began to understand each other better, we both gave in to each other's needs and wants. I will be the first to omit that I have been at fault based on my attitude and lack of leadership in handling each mini-crisis that we have experienced over the years. I have to give credit to Lin for assuming the spiritual leadership role many times during our marriage turbulence. God's protective and healing hand has always been with us in our good and bad times. Without him, we would have fallen apart a long time ago.

My short stay at Fort Gordon would soon expire and my beautiful bride and I would be off to Fort Stewart. Finally, I would be out of the barracks that I share with two other roommates. The space sure was tight! I was glad to be able to move into a larger space. We ended up renting another trailer in an even smaller trailer park. Our landlord happened to be a Christian man. We have not kept in touch over the years and the last I heard about him his wife had passed away and he remarried in his very late years. I hope he is still plugging away because he was a huge inspiration to us and a great mentor to me. I find it quite interesting that those who have had the biggest influence on my Christian life have been those who have been informal leaders. Just everyday people fighting in the trenches of life doing their best to honor God and his will which does not surprise me one bit.

A Soldier's Progress

1 Corinthians 1:27-29 But God hath chosen the foolish things of the world to confound the wise; and God hath chosen the weak things of the world to confound the things which are mighty; And base things of the world, and things which are despised, hath God chosen, yea, and things which are not, to bring to nought things that are: That no flesh should glory in his presence.

The first church we attended while stationed at Fort Stewart was a local Independent Baptist Church that I found while I was single and living in the barracks. I had attended only one other church prior that I was invited to on my way to the Post Exchange when I first arrived at Stewart. It was very much different than anything else I have ever been used to. There may have been a little more wind sucking than I ever heard before but I still managed to make it through the message. I suppose what through me for a loop was the tongue speaking at the end. It felt like a cool wind came in the room with an eerie feeling that kind of spooked me. If someone wants to speak in an unknown tongue before God that it is between them and God. I have definitely seen people do a whole lot worse in the name of God that is for sure. I do not know that many people being rushed to the hospital or killed for babbling words that are not understood.

1 Corinthians 14:19   Yet in the church I had rather speak five words with my understanding, that by my voice I might teach others also, than ten thousand words in an unknown tongue.

Anyways, the person that invited me to the service did a follow up visit with me and I took him through the Scripture that I had questions about concerning some of the church's activities. After our conversation he felt that I had some valid points that he did not have all the answers for, so he had his pastor call me. The conversation had not gone very far before he started to get irate and stated, "If you were a true Christian you would know that this was the right church!" He was on the border line of cursing me out! I politely ended the call and future experiences with churches of this type. Even so, I am sure there were some God fearing and loving people within those church walls of my bad experience. I have not found it possible to lump them all in a heresy pile because of one person, even if it was the pastor.

I did find a place of worship that I was more familiar with. It was a small IFB church that was pastored by a veteran whom I believed served at Fort Stewart also. He was interesting to say the least. I felt as though he was trying fit in with a particular brand of preachers such as the southern type who dress a little flashy, shout, use excessive Amens, and who kick an occasional flower pot. The problem was that this preacher was from New York and you could tell he was faking a southern accent or at least it sounded fake to me. This type of "fakeness" does not sit well with me. As a matter of fact I can not stand it, more so now than I did then. The sad reality is that it is everywhere and within every denomination. I suppose he was doing what he felt he needed to do to get noticed by these types of preachers. Of course, I could be completely wrong on my assessment. But, for whatever reason I seem to spot out when someone attempts to be someone they are not. Some call it discernment.

Searching for IFB churches became a battle drill. A battle drill is a military action that is conducted without thinking. For instance, when a soldier hears incoming artillery rounds fired at his unit's location the soldier immediately without thinking shouts out, "INCOMING, a clock position, and a distance for the unit to run in." The unit is so conditioned to the drill that they too respond without thought so they can arrive to a position of safety. The IFB church became my initial battle drill because it was in the IFB church that I enlisted in God's service and was the unit I found safety with. The problem is that IFB churches tend to preach that the INCOMING rounds are launched from other various local churches making them the enemy.

Here lies the invisible chains of power and control even to the point where some would question the salvation of other denominations because of variance in doctrine. The problem I had with this and where questions began to surface were due to the fact that I am a soldier in the U.S. Army. As a soldier, I have had the opportunity to meet Christians from various denominational backgrounds who happen to have a strong and deeply rooted love for the Lord and his Word.

I would later understand and realize that God places people where he wants. For example, I think of Martin Luther who was a product of the Roman Catholic Church. Even after he came to the saving knowledge of Jesus Christ by faith alone he had no desire to leave the Catholic Church, he simply desired for it to be reformed. It seems to be clear to me that the Lord had allowed these differences to exist to prevent another Tower of Babel religious system with the attempt and intention of making a name for itself. Think about it, if everyone did everything the exact same way here on earth, especially with our sinful nature, we would be in a religious bureaucratic mess unlike we have ever seen. Nevertheless, the IFB church I initially attended was one of the first stops of my spiritual journey as a new soldier in Christ and in the U.S. Army. We had met some good people at the church, but after a period of time we felt that we should check out another church not very far away. By this time we were able to get to know my landlord and his wife better.

Why the King James Bible?

One of the reasons we kept with these IFB churches is because of the consistent use of the King James Bible. It is not hard or difficult for me to accept or believe that God would preserve his Word in the English language considering that English is spoken worldwide

Psalms 12:6-7 The words of the LORD are pure words: as silver tried in a furnace of earth, purified seven times. Thou shalt keep them, O LORD, thou shalt preserve them from this generation for ever.

This truth alone impressed upon my heart that God has preserved his Word for the English speaking people without error. I am not saying that God will not use other versions; as a matter of fact my uncle was saved by reading another version. He now stands by the KJV for some if not all of the same reasons I do. The reality is there are not a whole lot of churches who follow this same train of thought. They either feel that it is the "best" translation (but only a translation,) or that it is one of equal inspiration to the others. To me that is confusion and we know that the Lord is not the author of confusion. I liked the K.I.S.S. method, "Keep It Simple Stupid!"

One of the issues faced with the IFB organizations today is the attitude of superior knowledge. This has even seeped into the area of Bible translations which has left a bad taste in the mouths of many. Many within the IFB movement have risen to state of Phariseeism in attitude and action, even using the KJV controversy as a spiritual measuring stick. Because of this, I myself struggled with thinking that others were less spiritual if they did not believe every point of doctrine in the same manner as I had come to understand it to include Bible translations. The complexity of the whole issue and discussion surfaces with all of the various degrees of understanding and play on words such as "preservation" and "inspiration."

In the past the KJV controversy has been one of the major deciding factors pertaining the churches we became members of; but, we do not make it a divisive issue when it comes to fellowship with other Christians. We have met and know may Christ loving Christian who use other versions of the Bible. God is using them in mighty ways. So if God loves them, we have absolutely no right to do otherwise. This train of thought and understanding would develop over time without the help of the IFB community due to the fear of openly speaking on such topics which could ultimately lead to shaming.

Why Change Churches?

Changing churches due to Army assignments and doctrinal differences allowed my wife and I to see the different personalities of churches. In Cleveland where I was saved, the church was traditional and reserved. The church where my wife grew up was loud and vibrant. The churches at Fort Stewart were a combination of the two. One thing common in all was the fact that the church's personality was often dictated by the pastor's personality and demeanor. Throughout these observations, I was beginning to understand my own spiritual personality and demeanor. I would hear people shout "Amen!" and felt as though I had to be just as outward in my expression to be accepted. I would later, as I do now, stand firm in my own expression which is more internal regardless of what congregation I am sitting in. I am who I am, which is how God made me. I do not need to impress anyone but God when it comes to my style of worship. Neither do I expect everyone else to express themselves in the same way. All I expect is for people to "keep it real."

Both of the IFB churches at Stewart we attended supported a Christian Military Service Home. This is where Lin and I experienced great times of fellowship from a house hosted by various IFB couples as missionaries. A couple of these families we were able to get to know and respect throughout our time at Stewart. We also were able to meet other Christian single soldiers and young couples that were around our age. I was glad to see other young Christians, many who were raised in the church, seeking to grow in their relationship with Christ and other believers, because I had seen many who used the Army as a way of escape to experience the world. This happens to be a huge prayer of mine for our own children. My heart would be filled with joy to know my children, two who are currently in the Army, had the opportunity to experience such fellowship and growth.

The Military Christian Service Home provided times of conversation, prayer, Bible study, food, and games. I am thankful for those who put together such an outreach platform and investment as this for our troops. It really gave me an opportunity to see other Christians in action outside of church walls. We were far from perfect, yet had a very common goal which was to be ambassadors for our faith. We would even formulate our own outreach missions amongst ourselves at the home. One day my wife, a couple of other soldiers, and I decided to street preach in front of Wal-Mart outside of the front gate. We held signs while Mike a bandsman played hymns on his trumpet. We also passed out Gospel tracts in the parking lot. Times such as these were exciting knowing we had planned and executed a spiritual operation for the glory of God.

While at Stewart I wanted everyone to know about my new found faith in Christ. I set out to witness to those within my unit and anyone on base that I could even if it meant passing out tracts on one of the base's corners. I was amazed at all the opportunities that the Lord gave me and many of them were in the field and I bunked with another soldier in a tent. I was in a Signal Battalion so once our equipment was set up, which I hated by the way especially putting up the camouflage netting. But once she was all set up we had quite a bit of free time on our hands and I would use this time to share the Gospel. I still have the Bible that I took with me to the field. It is rather used now with a whole lot of 100 mile an hour tape (better known as duck tape.) I even wrote some of the names I had the opportunity to witness to and see saved. Not all responded so enthusiastically. Some responded in the manner of Agrippa or even mocked the Gospel.

*Acts 26:28 Then Agrippa said unto Paul,
Almost thou persuadest me to be a Christian.*

My ministry at this stage of my journey was definitely in the spiritual trenches on the hillsides of life which would even define my ministry today. I did not have a church office with a beautiful church building filled with a host of congregants which happened to be my erroneous thought of what the ministry should and ought to be. It would take many years after my time at Stewart for me to understand this.

I was glad to have met other spiritual trench-fighters during this time while serving with the 3rd Infantry Division to include my landlord. These are the people I learned the most from and bonded with. For some reason I have never been able to bond with formal clergy. If anything, my perception has been that I have been seen more as a threat. I never sought for myself to be at odds with the formal clergy I came in contact with. It was just my desire to know the truth even if that meant standing against system they held dear. Why? Because many of the clergy especially within IFB churched depend on the giving of their congregations for financial support. In other words their paycheck and benefits come from the church. I have absolutely no issues with this accept when you have to compromise to get it or maintain it.

This compromise usually involves building walls and creating protective barriers. It also involves identifying potential threats. Now it is one thing to identify potential wolves who would harm the flock, but it a completely whole other matter when the pastor is protecting his pocket book regardless what happens to the sheep. I understand this to be a quite natural fleshly response because we must provide for our family. However, I have come to the conclusion if it comes down to compromising in this manner I would assume it to be better to get a secular job while continuing to work the ministry.

Compromise was an issue and it had an impact on us moving between the two churches we did at Stewart. We actually felt led to move back to the first church after one of the Military Christian home directors became pastor. We felt the return was necessary because of the dishonesty of the pastor from the church we decided to leave. As mentioned earlier, in the IFB community the KJV issue is a huge platform. The dishonest pastor was not completely honest with us concerning our agreement on the issue and ended up lying to appease others within the community and the IFB bureaucracy.

Our return to the church with the pastor I respected, I

knew he did not consider himself to be a member of the IFB bureaucracy. At least I never got that impression. I really felt that he cared about our spiritual development. He even allowed me to preach from the pulpit. I still remember to this day of how nervous I was. I was preaching along and reached a point where my mind went blank. The silence seemed as if it were an eternity and this I stated, "I hate when this happens!" which made it even worse. Somehow, I managed to finish the sermon and was thankful to this pastor for the opportunity share what God laid upon my heart regardless of how poorly I delivered it.

People seemed to be touched by the sermon, not because of its delivery but because of who it was delivered by. My nerves have caused me to cry out to God for the boldness and strength to preach his Word. I would tell the Lord even if I only spoke two words for his glory, as long as he is glorified that is all that matters to me and those would be the most blessed sermons even to this day. It is those that I "think" that I got licked are the ones I really bomb on and seem to have no impact. My nerves were also challenged by the Army while I was preparing for Special Forces training.

Special Forces

In 1997, I had trained up for the possibility of becoming a Green Beret for months. Thankfully my unit was very supportive by allowing me to train during our scheduled physical fitness time in the mornings. I would fill up my rucksack with 50 lbs or more and hit the road. All of the training helped me greatly when I arrived to SFAS (Special

Forces Assessment and Selection.) I ended up making it all the way to the second day of team week which was the hardest thing I ever did in my life. I had never put so many miles on these feet and so much weight on my back my entire life until this point. Health wise I was fine, I just was not mentally sold on the idea of making a future with the Green Beret's. I just did not have peace about it.

In March of 1997, just prior to leaving for SFAS, my wife's father Larry was killed by a drunk driver. Even so, I set out for the selection course not long after his funeral which was not a great time for her or me to continue with the process. So instead of completing the course and risking the temptation of answering a successful completion, I told my team that I was going to complete the day's activities and respectfully withdraw. They appreciated the extra help for the day and understood where I was coming from. When I spoke with the cadre 1SG before leaving he said I did great and was welcome to come back.

I felt bad for withdrawing. I felt like I worked very hard for it and failed. But deep down inside I knew God had a plan. Instead of meditating and seeking God for consolation bought a six pack of beer to help me relax and fall asleep that evening. When I returned home I told my wife what happened and she was a little disappointed that I drank the beer considering her understandable disdain for alcohol which led to the death of her father. So from that point I decided to leave alcoholic beverages alone to be a good example for my children and so that I would not be an excuse for someone else's drunkenness. Besides, I have seen enough alcohol abuse in my own family to last a lifetime.

Isaiah 5:11 Woe unto them that rise up early
in the morning, that they may follow strong drink; that
continue until night, till wine inflame them!

Deployment

While at Fort Stewart I spent quite a bit of time in the field and I also deployed to the Middle East in support of Operation Southern Watch in 1998. I did not know what to expect from the deployment, only that we could be going to war with Iraq. The hardest part of the deployment was not doubt saying goodbye to my wife and two little ones. The deployment lasted around five months before we returned home. It was definitely a different experience for me because this was my first time overseas seeing a new culture. Hearing the prayer music from the towers and seeing toilets mounted in the floor was enough for me to appreciate the freedoms and luxury we enjoy everyday in the states.

I was fortunate to be able to call home regularly which I enjoyed very much. Also one of the air bases we stayed at had and air conditioned chapel which I found relief from the scorching heat. Even the shade was hot! It was also nice to be able to meditate on God's goodness and to plan different ways to be able to share the Gospel. We actually had some good Army chaplains on the deployment which provided outstanding fellowship. One day we were having a Bible study and one of the chaplains stated that there was nothing wrong with having a cold beer every so often. I felt led to bring up a point about weak brothers using him as an excuse for their drunkenness. He really had no response because I believe he understood what I was saying.

New Assignment Orders

My few years at Stewart would soon come to a close towards the end of the summer of 1998. I had decided to reenlist in the Army as an Infantryman. Even though I did not pursue Special Forces I wanted to do something high speed so the next best thing for me was the Infantry. Plus, I was able to select my next duty assignment that allowed me to be stationed with my brother at Fort Campbell. My Signal Battalion commander looked at me like I was an idiot when I told her that I was changing my job to Infantry while she was handing me an Army medal for our deployment to the Middle East. She knew there was sense in trying to talk me out of it because I am sure she knew what my response would be- It is God's will. It is sort of hard to argue anything with someone who makes this statement. In all reality, what could you really say?

SCREAMING EAGLES

We ended up moving our rather new single-wide mobile home to a small town outside of Ft. Campbell, Kentucky. Yes, another trailer park! I still question myself as to where that trailer we moved to three states fits into the will of God for our life. The only thing I can figure out is that I should have prayed about it before the rather skilled salesman took advantage of our youth. It is what it is I suppose- a thorn is my side. Even so, I trust that God even has a plan for this aspect of our lives. It was not all that bad and I would choose the worst of housing conditions to keep the family and animals that I have. Our space will a little confined which put a little more restriction of my buddy Samson. Ole Samson was our half Great Dane and half Bull Mastiff. He was an awesome dog! He had a great temperament and was great with the kids. They could do just about what they wanted to him and it would not phase him a bit. He was so big they even rode on him a few times.

Infantry Training

Before I was able to report to Fort Campbell I had to attend OSUT (One Stop Unit Training). Thankfully I did not have to attend the Basic Training portion again which is part of OSUT.. I was inserted into the AIT (Advanced Individual Training) Infantry portion which was fine by me. The Drill Sergeants treated me with respect and even gave me time in the evening to go to the Entertainment center across the street from our barracks at Fort Benning. Other prior service soldiers were not so fortunate. There were other Specialists and even a Sergeant who went to other platoons who had to shave their heads with the other trainees and did not get the privileges that I did. One of my drill sergeants asked me how long I had been in at that point and I told him over four years. He said, "Man! You have been in almost as long as us!" Then he began to tell me what he expected of me while I was there which was basically to help them lead the soldiers within the platoon considering I was a promotable Specialist at the time.

I could not wait to finish training and earn my blue cord which only the Infantry wears. I also knew that I would have enough promotion points when I was awarded my new MOS Military Occupational Skill of 11B Infantryman. I longed to be able to wear those hard stripes and lead soldiers as a Sergeant. Training went well, except during a road march I partially tore my achilles tendon. This was not a good thing considering that I was planning on becoming a part of my brother's Pathfinder unit. He was already stationed at Fort Campbell and was the reason I requested to be assigned their as part of my reenlistment. I was still able to complete all the requirements for graduation but it was scary to think that I could have permanently damaged myself.

I was amazed at all of the opportunities I had to share my faith during training. The same Drill Sergeant that granted me the privileges listened to me as I shared with him portions of my spiritual journey and purpose while on a road march. I also met another prior service soldier who I got along with great. He was a Catholic, but he had absolutely no problem listening to my preaching. I can not remember his name today, but I do pray that the seeds that were planted in those two months of training have taken root in all of their lives.

The greatest part of graduation was seeing my wife and kids again. We visited the Infantry museum which was a blast. Since then they have built a new museum which I am itching to visit. We know a missionary to the military whose ministry is on Fort Benning and he has told us we need to see it. After graduation my leave would soon be finished and I sign into the 101st Airborne Division (Screaming Eagles) where I was assigned to Charlie Company 3/187 Infantry Regiment (Rakkasans). I was sent to a regular line unit due to my tendon injury which healed up not long after my arrival.

I heard stories about the Rakkasans as soon as I got to the reception battalion to sign in. They said that out of all the Infantry units on Campbell I was getting sent to the toughest unit which was fine by me. It is either all or nothing for me so I was looking forward to it. I was particularly intrigued by the "Battle Hair" they spoke of, which was strips of burlap sack that were carefully placed on our Kevlar helmets to give us a ferocious look. Yes, the battle hair combined with the camouflage paint on our face did make us look rather ferocious.

I had a huge leadership challenge upon my arrival to the Rakkasans which was addressed immediately by my First Sergeant during my in processing. He told me that even though I was a newly promoted Sergeant assigned to the Infantry, for the first time, he wanted me to lead my troops as if I had been in the Infantry from the beginning. That I did! I was one of the toughest leaders in our platoon. Maybe too tough at times which was a result of a little power placed in the hands of a young leader. These would prove to very valuable leadership lessons that I would learn later and reflect upon how ignorant I was about true leadership.

Air Assault School

I was only signed in for a couple of weeks before I was notified that I was to attend the Sabalauski Air Assault School. The rumor was that it was the toughest ten days in the Army. Honestly, I feel that I had spent ten tougher days elsewhere but it still was a physical and mental challenge. I would have to say that I hated the "Weaver" the most. It was an obstacle that I had to weave my body in and out of wooden beams going up and then going back down. It would be an obstacle that I would have to ace more than once throughout future training. Graduation day soon arrived and I was thankful to have been able to earn my first permanent badge to go on my Battle Dress Uniform (BDU's). After all one of the reasons I wanted to go Infantry was so that I could attend some high speed schools. Air Assault school was a great start.. When it came to badges I would never catch up my brother Sean who was assigned to the Pathfinder unit. He ended up earning his Airborne Badge, Pathfinder Badge, and Combat Infantryman Badge and Ranger Tab to add to his collection to name just a few and he is currently serving as a Brigade Command Sergeant Major. I ended up adding an Expert Infantryman Badge, Drill Sergeant, and Recruiting Badge to mine.

Pre-Ranger Course

One of the badges that my brother Sean and I set out to earn together was the Ranger Tab. Not long after I completed Air Assault school I was on my way to Pre-Ranger school which was a two week intensive course intended to ensure a high success rate at Ranger school. It costs quite a bit of funds to send a soldier to Ranger school and the last thing a soldier wants to do is waste these funds and be sent back to his Infantry unit with his head down.

I ended up attending the course with my squad leader. It was nice to at least know someone while at this grueling course. It definitely did not give me any added advantage though. I actually had a disadvantage that I should have kept to myself which was that I had not always been Infantry. As usual it seemed that I had identified myself to not be one of the "boys." There were some brigade long range division troops that had attended the course and they made sure they stuck together. I had made the mistake of letting them know I used to be Signal (Communications,) got into a verbal altercation with them, and managed to get in a verbal match with one of the instructors. All which equaled to no good concerning my graduation fate.

One night, we returned from a patrol and some of us had to pull guard that night. One of the long range troops was sleeping and I put him on the spot about it. Ironically, I was put on the spot for the same exact thing by an instructor the following night and I responded in a similar negative matter except I told the instructor that he was not going to use profanity when speaking to me. He simply walked away. He had a fix for me! The next day I was assigned the job of the Bravo team leader in my squad. One of the Bravo team leader's responsibilities was to put together the supply list which included chow (food.) All I had to do was get with the previous Bravo team leader and copy the supply list and turn it is. I did exactly that and reported on time to the head shed. I banged on the door and heard "Who is it!" I replied with my name, position, and what I was there for. Then all I heard was crickets! I knocked again and still crickets! Needless to say I ended up returning back to my squad with the bad news that there was no chow and believe me, they were not happy at all.

I ended up making it through the entire course and at the end we had to rate our peers. If someone fell below a 70% from the peers they were dropped from the course and it had to be completed all over again. My name was called to report to the head shed for my fate. The head instructor in a smirking kind of way said "I am sorry you have received a 69% by your peers, you are going to have to complete the course again." This struck me hard and I thought to myself "Lord, why?" Going back to my unit was the toughest part. I realize that I often fall short, but I do want to do my best to bring glory to my God by my actions and performance. I continue to learn that it is not about whether we fail or succeed in a particular goal, it is how we respond to failure or success that matters. God uses both outcomes to mold and shape us. God has an expected end for our lives. This is why I often state that I am just a passenger on the bus which is a Heavenly vehicle that has a predetermined route that only the Driver knows. He knows all of the bumps, twists, and turns.

After this experience I was determined not to return to

Ranger school at all. I started to think and pray about exactly what the Lord would have me do. One course of action was to re-enlist to change my job but the doors were not opening. Another was to reenlist and stay an Infantryman with a pinpoint assignment, but those doors were not opening either. However, the doors were opening for me to finish my contract so that I could attend Bible College and secular college. My initial thoughts were that I could combine my passion as a soldier for the U.S. Army and a soldier of Jesus Christ into one work which would seem to fit perfectly and that was to become an Army Chaplain. I had to be sure that is what the Lord wanted me to do, so I did not throw away the other courses of action. At one point, I thought the door for reenlisting as an Infantryman was still plausible due to the fact that I was faced with Ranger School once again.

My brother Sean was scheduled to attend the next Pre-Ranger school class and he wanted me to attend with him. At first I told him absolutely not! However he was persistent and eventually convinced me that I should attend with him. If it were not for him I most definitely probably would not have attended. So there we found ourselves taking our physical fitness tests in order to get into the course. The PT test was basically a mirror finish from the first time I attended except for the sit-ups. For some reason the grader was not counting all of my sit-ups and when the event was complete he stated I had fallen short and sent me back to the back of the line to retake the event. I was already a little fatigued and thought it would be impossible to do them over again. I asked the Lord for strength and managed to complete the requirement. I was then faced with my next challenge which was the pull-ups.

A Soldier's Progress

The pull-up was definitely my challenge as it was with many others. If we failed that particular event we were still permitted to attend the course under the condition that the event was successfully completed at the end of the course. This was a lot of pressure knowing that we could have met all of the other course requirements only to be sent back to our unit for failure to meet the pull-up standard. I had to work my behind off throughout the course in order to accomplish this physical challenge. Thankfully, I was able to do so both times. However, an even bigger obstacle had to be the fact that I had to face the same instructors from the previous class that made sure I would have to return if I was to have a shot at the actual school. Even while I was running the 2 mile run event the instructor I had a confrontation with saw that I had red running shoes and shouted out "Look at those ruby red slippers!" I figured for sure that the class was going to be a long one. By the way, I can kick myself a thousand times for buying those red running shoes. I hated them and was too cheap and cashless to buy a new pair, so I just colored them with a black permanent marker.

The good news story about this class with my brother is that we led the way throughout the course which impressed the instructors. It was a great feeling to be able to run at the front of the pack during the 5 mile grueling run that the whole class was not fond of at all! The fastest instructors smoked our bags; but, we managed to keep up and still lead the formation. This earned a great deal of respect from our instructors along with an opportunity I had to preach the Gospel at the course. The Chaplain was not able to make it to our Sunday worship opportunity, so I volunteered to conduct the service. The students and instructors were in awe. One of them approached me after the service as said they would never see me as they did before and were glad I stepped up to the plate. Even the instructors did not look at me the same afterwards and their respect had increased. My brother and I graduated with flying colors and we were scheduled to attend the actual Ranger School course soon afterwards. God had a plan for my return to the Pre-Ranger course.

Campbell Church Hunting

While assigned to Fort Campbell my family and I immediately went on the hunt for a local Bible believing church. We ended up finding a small Independent Baptist Church in Hopkinsville, Kentucky. We had visited a church to two previous to this one but ended up being members at the Hopkinsville location. The church was roughly thirty minutes from our residence which was often challenging especially when attending services twice on Sunday and on Wednesday night. We developed a solid relationship with the pastor and his wife which would last for years. Our friendship was based on the common doctrinal interest and understanding we had. We would often fellowship on these points especially while visiting the community each Saturday as we went door to door sharing the Gospel. The areas we disagreed on we did not discuss, probably because we knew it would put a roadblock on our conditional relationship. I would not realize that our relationship was conditional until years later down the road when the Lord called us to plant The Soldier's

Sanctuary.

As I reflect on our relationship, I am not all that shocked to see that it fizzled out. I appreciate the zeal the pastor has, in many respects it is not according to knowledge, especially when his knowledge in measured in conditional love. I mention this with no ill will at all towards him or his family. I feel that he has allowed himself to become victim of a religious system that has gone bankrupt. A conditional conditional religious system that will only accept you if your follow their rules in the manner they describe. If you follow the rules and play the part then you are "loved" and respected. If you go against their rules and do not play the part you are excommunicated, not loved, rejected, and ignored. This behavior happens to be the antithesis of what it means to be a Christian which is clearly shown Matthew 18:23-35.

Romans 10:2 For I bear them record that they have a zeal of God, but not according to knowledge.

Matthew 18:32-33 Then his lord, after that he had called him, said unto him, O thou wicked servant, I forgave thee all that debt, because thou desiredst me: Shouldest not thou also have had compassion on thy fellowservant, even as I had pity on thee?

God has never forsaken me or left me in the dust! So which of my brethren feel they have the right to do the same? This is an area that I strive to be conscious of. I realize that I am only one person and can only give so much attention to so many people. I also realize that this is the reality for those that have forsaken my family and I. However, when a person stops returning a simple gesture as a Christmas card and will not respond to the cards we send on a yearly basis we know that there is an issue. This is the same preacher I called when the Soldier's Baptist church began. I wanted him to know what God had called us to do and was interested in his feedback. All of the feedback was good, but was in a hesitant manner that is for sure. I ended the conversation with our new website which was hosted on MySpace when many were using it for social media. One of the features of the sight was to play music in the background. I had a contemporary music song from the band *Third Day* playing which I believe was all that was needed to sever our relationship. I thought this would be a possibility considering that he felt that anything with a drum was Satanic. So it was, I was written off as having joined the dark side I suppose due to my genre of Christian music.

While attending this same church my brother Sean came to know the Lord while we were sitting at my house discussing the Scripture and Salvation. At the time he was experiencing some rather turbulent relationship issues and was looking for answers pertaining to life in general. I was ecstatic that my brother accepted Christ as his Savior! I saw an immediate change with a desire to be more like Christ. Soon after his profession of faith I brought him to our church. I wanted to immediately start going over some discipleship basics with him in another room of the church during Sunday School. After the service the same day the pastor approached me with practically gnashing teeth and basically stated that was not how business was conducted there. My brother never returned after that and maybe he was the smarter man for doing so. After I calmed down a bit I gave him the benefit of the doubt and continued to drive on.

Sean found another local church to attend where he was baptized. He would soon after receive orders for Italy where he would eventually marry an Italian woman and have two children. We do not speak to each other all that often but one spiritual conversation I remember having with Sean when he was in Italy between deployments. He told me, "Andy, I have not forgotten anything you have taught me". Those words and the notes my brother wrote me to include one that he inscribed in a Bible and one he sent from Basic Training have encouraged me even until this day.

Hebrews 13:1,5   Let brotherly love continue....
Let your conversation be without covetousness; and be
content with such things as ye have: for he hath said, I will
never leave thee, nor forsake thee.

The real issue was power and control which is rampant in many of these like churches and if anything or anyone attempts to go against their power and control they become a marked man or woman. I can not say for sure if I was marked or not by this pastor at the time. After all there were only a couple of families attending the church at the time, so if he marked me there would not be many more to minister to. In no way am I saying this man is the spawn of the devil. All I am saying is that his righteousness amounts to the same as yours and mine. The problem with many of these leaders is that they feel as if they see above the rest of the congregation which is furthest from the truth. We are all equal team members with an equal calling based on the gifts and talents that the Lord has given us. Nevertheless, I did enjoy the spiritual conversation that we shared during our time of service at this church. I do recognize that we all make mistakes so I have never held any of the negativity I saw against him. I am just sad that he has held petty opinionated preferences as mark of division.

On a positive not with a minor irritation my oldest son was baptized at this church in a horse trough which I thought was a unique experience for our family. Judah wasn't yet 4 years old when he called upon Jesus to save him. Even at such a young age I felt that Judah understood the basic concept of his sin and the need for a Savior. I was to honored that we had the conversation together and was able to pray together concerning his salvation. I told our pastor of Judah's salvation decision which was hard for him to swallow. So before he would commit to baptizing Judah he wanted to interview him first. At first I was a little irritated because I felt like my judgment as his father was being blown off. If I felt that my son did not know what he was doing I would have not asked for him to be baptized. Nevertheless I agreed to the interview which Judah passed with flying colors. We must not forget that the Lord said to not suffer the little ones to come unto him. I am convinced with all of my heart that if a little one calls upon God for salvation that God not only hears the child, but he saves the child.

My wife battled with this growing up due to over zealous preachers attempting to earn another feather for their hat.

After their drawn out invitations that I have heard I was have tempted myself to go forward just so they would sing the hundredth stanza of Just As I Am. I believe my wife was saved the first time she called upon the Lord for salvation and the one or two times two follow were just reassurance of her initial commitment whether someone erroneously claimed that her subsequent prayers were the initial ones.

We would end up leaving this church on a good note upon my exit from the regular Army. They seen us off with a small going away party and a very nice gift which was a framed page from an antique King James Bible which we have hanging on our wall today. It has been many years since I have heard anything from this brother. We make a point to continue to send a Christmas card on a yearly basis to his house regardless. There are others that we send cards to also. It is our way to let them know that we still love them and our door is always open. Lin and I realize that is our responsibility to pray and care for those who treat us this way. After all, this is the manner in which God treats us. If I received what I deserved I would have been smashed like a bug and forsaken years ago. Yet God's love endures forever!

THE SOUTH

I had no idea what to expect, I just spent the last seven years of my life on active duty with the United States Army. I knew I would miss being a soldier so when I sat down with the in service recruiter to look at my options for after leaving active duty, I decided to stay in the Army Reserve. The recruiter asked me what I wanted to do and after a moment of silence he piped up with "How about becoming a Drill Sergeant?" I said, "I will take it!" Now for the big move to the Palmetto State. We decided a while back that we wanted to return to my wife's home territory so we bought a few acres of land. We had also purchased a single wide mobile home when we were stationed back at Fort Stewart which would now be on its second move. In order for us to get refinancing we wanted as a land home package we had to put a permanent foundation with footers which we did.

We finally made it to our new home and to my amazement considering we were out in the boonies was that as I sat in my truck waiting for our mobile home arrive I noticed our neighbor came outside to place his trash on the curb. I looked a little close and I could not believe it! It was my squad leader from way back at Fort Stewart. He had exited the Army before I left Stewart and I figured he returned to Michigan where he was from. But no, he ended up across the street from me!

Our neighbor was a great help to us. He assisted me with building a deck for our trailer and made himself available for anything else we needed. I was glad that we were able to get along. I was unsure at first because he was a leader that was not exactly sure how to respond around me especially with my aggressiveness with the things of God.

As for church we were already set on where we were going to attend. We really did not give it much thought or prayer. For some reason we felt there was no other "church alive" in the area so we attended the church where I met my wife and where the motto was "a church alive is worth the drive." This is also where I was getting prepared to attend Bible college.

Lin and I quickly found jobs which was a huge blessing. I found a job working pest control and delivering pizza and Lin found a job waitressing. She also delivered pizza for a little while to while I was taking classes at a local university later down the road. No matter our circumstances God provided our every need.

The summer of 2001 was also an exciting one because the arrival of our first daughter Jacquelin (Jacky-Lin) was in the queue of our life also. We sure were excited about our new little one's arrival and so were her brothers Judah and Jesse. God had not only provided for our needs he was filling our quiver with precious little ones. On July, 27, 2001 our little Jacky-Lin was born.

This first summer not in the active Army was a packed one that is for sure. We had a huge move, needed to find jobs, a house to get set up, a baby to be born, college to register for, and a new Army Reserve unit to report to. The Lord made it all seamless or at least it seemed that way anyway. We could have not done all that needed to be done without teamwork that is for sure.

One day I reported to the pest control job that I had on

September 11, 2001 and was making my rounds to our customers and the only door I remember knocking on was that of a woman who answered the door in complete horror and silence. I asked here if anything was wrong and she immediately responded with "Do you know what just happened?" I told the lady I did not and she replied "Come in" and took me to her television set. The images soon brought me to the horrific state of this woman and we both stared at the television set trying to decipher we were watching.

As I saw the planes hit the towers the only thing I could say was "We are going to war!" I do not remember much of anything else besides returning to the office unable to complete anymore work for the day. I knew that my Rakkasan Infantry unit I had just left would be in preparation for any orders they may imminently receive. Oh how much I wanted to be with them to avenge the atrocity that was committed against our people on that day.

This would not be the only time I wrestled with these feelings. These same feelings would transition to the desire to be with my combatant brothers in this time of war, but God would close the doors on these feelings multiple times. Even so I have always accepted God's plans and have come to the realization that God has called me to fight in the spiritual trenches up until this point. This being said, if I must pick up my weapon once again to defend this country and people; I am ready, willing, and know this is what I have been trained for.

If I never have to use my training in a combat situation it still has not been without use. I have used my military training in all aspects of my life to include the ministry. There are so many parallels between military service and service in God's Army which I have spelled out multiple times in my sermons and writing.

Even though I preached at the local county jail I vividly remember preparing a five minute sermon for a Bible college requirement. I sure was nervous! My college peers that I was preparing to preach to where for the most part southern-bread, hanky-waving, shouting preachers who had opposite personalities than myself. I refused to be anything other than who God made me and I was preparing to preach in the style that God built me for regardless if they liked it or not.

I really never did fit in with the "Southern Crew" for some reason. For the most part I was just a "Yankee", or at least I felt that way. I did not really allow this to bother me much because I was not there for anyone else but God. So I prepared my sermon with the intention to be used by the Spirit of the Living God to inspire and motivate my fellow Bible students.

I do not have a copy of this sermon but I do remember the key element which was a variation of the Ranger's Creed I created called the Christian's Creed. Even though I did not graduate from Ranger school, this is a creed that I recited multiple times a day during the months I spent at the school. The words have stuck with me to this day and I have applied many of these same principles to my spiritual life. My version the "Christian Creed" follows the "Ranger Creed".

Christian Creed

Recognizing that I volunteered as a Christian, fully

knowing the hazards of my chosen calling, I will always endeavor to uphold the prestige, honor, and high esprit de corps of my local church.

Acknowledging the fact that a Christian is an elite soldier who arrives at the cutting edge of spiritual battle by land, sea, or air, I accept the fact that as a Christian my country expects me to move further, faster and pray harder than any other soldier.

Never shall I fail my brethren. I will always keep myself mentally alert, spiritually strong and morally straight and I will shoulder more than my share of the task whatever it may be, one-hundred-percent and then some.

Gallantly will I show the world that I am a specially selected and well-trained soldier. My courtesy towards other men and women of God, study of God's Word, and care of the church shall set the example for others to follow.

Energetically will I meet the enemies of my God. I shall defeat them on the field of battle for I am better trained and will fight with the hand of God. Surrender is not a Christian word outside of surrender to God. I will never leave a fallen comrade to fall into the hands of the enemy and under no circumstances will I ever embarrass my Lord.

Readily will I display the intestinal fortitude required to fight on to the Lord's objective and complete the mission though I be the lone survivor.

If you noticed, only a few words needed exchanged due to the great parallels which exist within this creed. I have found this to be so with many of the military creeds I have recited over the years. During delivery of this message I was sure to stand at the position of attention and shout just as I did the Ranger Creed at Ranger school. Every eye in the college classroom was carefully fixed upon my recitation. I am not sure that anyone in the class even blinked.

As for Bible college, I honestly expected a whole lot more than what I experienced. If anything I feel as though I learned more of what not to do versus what to do. This caused me to question some things which I do not feel was received all that well. Good or bad, God was teaching me many things and I was taking notes.

One of the questions I had which the senior pastor proved was concerning how the invitation was given at the conclusion of services. It was not out of the ordinary for an invitation to be 15-20 minutes long at least. Emotions would be worked up during this time and people would eventually respond. The question I asked pertaining to this practice was "Preacher, where in the Bible do we see this type of invitation given?" The preacher responded, "I am not sure, I have never been asked that question." Do not get me wrong I have used an invitation at the conclusion of services myself. However, if someone is under conviction by the Holy Spirit throughout the service they will be asking the question "Sir, what must I do to be saved?" This type of response I see in the Bible.

This type of behavior from what I see originates from a "legitimacy by results" mentality. In order to meet the legitimacy standard one must prove by the numbers that they are legitimate. In other words going back to the "feather in the cap" ideology I mentioned earlier. It is perceived by many that if a person does not come forward with some type of decision that the service was a failure in a sense. My only problem with this is- why are we at church in the first place? If it is to pray, sing spiritual songs, and worship God; I am not sure where the "We must see results mentality originates from". After all, does not God give the increase? We have nothing to prove to include our legitimacy if we are legitimate in the eyes of God.

There is no doubt in my mind that God put me exactly where he wanted me for training purposes. There was much to learn concerning how things should be done and how things should not be done. In all reality the whole learning process which never ends is necessary for our spiritual growth and proves over and over our individual feebleness and imperfection. I am far from perfect and have no right to judge the hearts and intentions of God's servants. I mention the positive and negatives from my experience to highlight our frailty and the fact that we all can learn from each other.

My formal Bible college experience would be short lived. However my true college experience continues on to today and will continue for the rest of my life. I am continually learning from the experiences and challenges that the Lord has put within the path that he has called me to. The Lord's will and way is truly unique as our fingerprints concerning his individual children. Therefore I respect the diversity found in the calling of others. This is a hard concept for many because they feel that all must have a similar path to theirs or it must not be the will of God.

My college experience did not end with Bible college, I enrolled in a local accredited university to pursue an eventual possibility of becoming a chaplain in the Army. I chose history for my major and enjoyed the courses very much. Many of the courses were the core basic classes that are normally completed within the first two years of study. One of those classes was English where I began to write more seriously. I took the opportunity to write about my faith. Not sure exactly how the content of my writing impacted my English professor, but he did say that he liked my style of writing.

It is amazing how positive feedback sticks with us for a very long time. Sometimes it is so easy to find ourselves focusing on the negative aspects of others and organizations. While there is a benefit towards identifying our weaknesses so that we can improve I am continually reminding myself that there must be a balance. During this time in my life there was a whole lot of balancing going on as I evaluated where my family and I should be at concerning the ministry.

Our vision began to become incompatible with the vision of the church we were attending. We felt that we were not a valued team member and we felt that we were just another number contributing to a crowd seeking entertainment. Of course this did not apply to all, we had quite a few genuine Christian friends whose hearts were set on worshipping God and their walks with him. Nevertheless, we felt inclined to pursue other opportunities of service which ended up being an expansion of spiritual training for us.

Drill Sergeant

During this time it was not long before that I completed Drill Sergeant School. I was called to active duty to serve as a Drill Sergeant which was fine for me for a couple of reasons. One, I was able to put to use all of those memorized Drill and Ceremony modules I agonizingly memorized while working my pest control job and two I was back to receiving a good paycheck with benefits as an active duty soldier.

My first duty as a Drill Sergeant was working with the soldiers at the Fort Jackson reception battalion. Basically our responsibility was to move soldiers from point A to point B as they processed into the Army. This is the place where soldiers complete all of their initial paperwork, get uniforms, and receive their medical shots prior to going to Basic Training.

I experienced some interesting moments while serving at Fort Jackson that I could say were unexpected, but then I can also say not expected because initial entry soldiers tend to do some crazy things due to not wanting to be there or they are just plain stupid period!

One day I was in the dining facility going through the line and there was a tall soldier in front of me putting his hand on top of the heads of other soldiers in the line as if he was blessing the or something. Before I was able to open my mouth to rip him a new one another Drill Sergeant who was assigned to the dining facility for the day came rushing in to deal with the soldier. Next thing I know, there is not just one Drill Sergeant there were multiple Drill Sergeants that flooded the dining facility to subdue this same soldier who was not only touching the heads of other soldiers but he had a lock in his hand that was postured like a weapon. This Drill Sergeants had no choice but to drag him out of the dining facility and slam him to the ground while waiting for the ambulance to arrive.

This was just an ordinary day at reception battalion where only God knew what was going to happen on any given day. My stay would only last a few weeks before I would be transferred to a new battalion that was testing a new extended physical fitness training program. This program put an additional month on each trainees Basic Training experience and its purpose was to see how well the program would improve and assist the soldiers with their physical well being and performance while in Basic Training and beyond.

Within this testing battalion and later within regular Basic Training units I was not the easiest or most mild mannered Drill Sergeant to say the least. I yelled a lot! I yelled so much that I had to pace myself so that I would not lose my voice. One day as I was on the verge of losing my voice I had an idea! Why don't I designate a Spokes Private? And so I did, I picked the loudest Private in the platoon and gave him instructions on his new duties and responsibility as a Spokes Private.

The very next day standing in front of the platoon I raised my hand and one finger pointed towards the open bay ceiling. This one finger signified, "BEAT YOUR FACE!" As soon as my Spokes Private seen the finger he yelled out at the top of his lungs, "BEAT YOUR FACE!" and immediately all the soldiers in the platoon assumed the front leaning rest position which is also known as the Push-Up. I too would assume the position with the soldiers as we as a team and unit would repetitiously knock out a series of push-ups in cadence and unison.

As a result of these repeated sayings and more, one day I arrived to the barracks unexpected and before reached the room I heard the platoon mimicking these sayings. I was quite honored by jesting of the soldiers because I knew the respected the professionalism and consistency I did my best to uphold at all times. But at the same time, I could not let them get off so easy and allow the opportunity for a good PT session to go by. That evening in that same room the temperature increased and the soldiers poured sweat as we did many push-ups, sit-ups, and scissor kicks. There is no doubt in my mind that all of the soldiers slept well that evening.

At the end of this same cycle when the soldiers were preparing to graduate this special test program and move on to Basic Training we were in a formation. During this formation the soldiers within our platoon wanted to recognize me and gave me a Drill Sergeant bear and a card. In the card it stated that they had the utmost respect for me and reiterated why they were mimicking my sayings on the day that I caught them. They said they wanted to be just like me, which are words that I will never forget!

I would carry these same sayings throughout my time as a Drill Sergeant and they became my signature. Some of the other Drill Sergeants were even jealous, especially when I was new arrival and we went out to the field where the soldiers were afforded a brief opportunity to perform skits. The first Drill Sergeant they selected was me and the other Drill Sergeants were shocked. They laughed, with a little bit of a jealous tone, and stated that it was quite impressive that I had impacted the soldiers in such a short period of time. All of this meant a great deal to me because I took the job extremely serious and I put some hard work in to get there.

My Drill Sergeant duties would soon end and totalled about a year on active status which is a year or two shorter than regular Army Drill Sergeants. I had nothing but respect for those who have endured the extended lengths of time performing this duty. The days were long, hard, and repetitive. It seems like an over glorified babysitting job at times, but when the soldiers thanked us at the end for molding and shaping them into better human beings and soldiers it made it all worth it.

Attention to Detail

Anyways, detail was the first thing I did when I hit the ground once again as a drill. One day I approached the morning formation from behind and noticed that one of the soldiers did not have his hands placed correctly behind the small of his back. I then quietly approached him from behind where he could not see me and began to commence a very loud on the spot correction which was close enough that there was absolutely no mistaking the verbal message that I was getting into his skull.

The soldier's learned rather quickly that there was not going to be very much I would miss, so they were sure to make sure their every move was locked and cocked. The passion and energy that I devoted to the troops earned the respect of the soldiers and my peers. This was important to me because I am always looking for an opportunity to share with others the reason I tick the way I do.

1 Peter 3:15 But sanctify the Lord God in your hearts: and be ready always to give an answer to every man that asketh you a reason of the hope that is in you with meekness and fear:

During this active duty tour I was able to share my story with my fellow drill sergeants on the way to a range one day. As we were conversing an opportunity arose where I was able to tell them about my previous active duty service and plan to become an Army chaplain.

Their response was very similar to the responses I received prior to this point and even today responses are pretty much the same. It gets very quiet with and an awkward silence followed by a "oh, I see". I guess many do not expect this type of language to proceed forth from my mouth even though I did not give them any other reason to think otherwise, except maybe my aggressiveness. I guess they figure that due to most Army chaplains being more meek and reserved, at least some of the were, that I would have behaved the same. If I were in their shoes then maybe I would; but I was not, I was a drill sergeant.

Besides up to that point in my career I has not been very impressed by the caliber of chaplains I experienced. I have seen all types to include those who smoke and use profanity. I will never forget the time I was standing in a battalion formation listening to a chaplain use a variety of profane words which not only stunned myself, but also stunned the unbelievers in my unit. One soldier told me, "I know I am the farthest from being a real believer, but this guy even offends me". This proved to me that even the lost expect so much more from Christians.

As for the overall drill sergeant duty the days were long and tiresome. Many people think that it is all about the yelling and control. The yelling got old after about two weeks. Even though I yelled a good bit I decided to pace myself and get assistance from the soldiers by holding up a number of fingers as a sign to them and they would shout the command. Drill Sergeant duty was a huge leadership lesson and valuable training to me. I started to see that leadership is not about me, it is about investing in others. This is an understanding that I am continually growing in.

My time would soon expire as a drill sergeant in 2004. On my last day I gathered my platoon together to sign my drill sergeant hat which I still have on my desk today. I was glad to be able to return to my family back in Ohio and start my new recruiting adventure which I speak of in the next chapter. However, before we look at this chapter I would like to mention an experience I had with some religious toilet paper during this same period of time.

Religious Toilet Paper

As a Drill Sergeant, I was in and out while attending our new church. I should have paid more attention when we first started attending when the pastor told me that the church was a "pastor led church". I assumed he was talking about leadership and not dictatorship. His style or pasturing proved to be the latter which was a huge leadership lesson for me on not how to lead.

One Sunday after a team of church members assisted a Bible printing missionary put together John/Romans booklets the pastor proclaimed from the pulpit- "I did not put together one John/Romans booklet! That is not my job! My Job is to supervise!!!" I looked over and saw the missionary as he shrank in the pew from embarrassment. I also look to see what the expression was on the face of my fellow soldiers who were in the congregation. We all knew what it means to lead from the front because that is what we have been trained to do our whole military career. They had the same reaction on their face as I did- "Did I just hear what I think I just heard!?"

This pastor obviously had some control issues. His arrogance eventually crumbled the church. This man did not even like to be challenged with evangelism. I asked him if he would like to gather a few men to go door to door and invite folks to church. He nastily replied "If that is what you want to do there are tracts on the wall, help yourself!" Again my reaction was disbelief and I questioned myself as to whether I heard what I just heard. We would have left much earlier except that I was busy with my deployment and did not have time to research other places of worship.

We all know what toilet paper is good for. As a matter of fact, if one goes too long without it there is a certain level of concern that will surely be experienced. However, there is a type of toilet paper that all of us can do without and that is religious toilet paper. Exactly what is "Religious Toilet Paper?"

Let me begin to answer that question with a true story. One day, many years ago, my wife called a certain pastor we were acquainted with to ask a question. For the purpose of this post I will name him Snuffy.

Snuffy: Hello!
My Wife: Hello, is Mr. Snuffy in?
Snuffy: Excuse me!?
My Wife: Oh! I am sorry! Is Pastor Snuffy in?
Snuffy: Excuse me!?
My Wife: Again I am sorry, do I have the wrong number?
Snuffy: It is DOCTOR Snuffy!!!

As soon as my wife told told me about this conversation I thought, "Well exccccuuuuuusssssseee me Snuffy!!!!" Then I wanted to put my Christianity on a shelf, call the man back, and give him a piece of my mind. Thankfully, I did not and realized that there were religious men who were stuck on stupid in the Bible and since the behavior of men has been rather consistent over time that means there are religious men who are stuck on stupid even today.

Matthew 23:5-12 But all their works they do for to be seen of men: they make broad their phylacteries, and enlarge the borders of their garments, And love the uppermost rooms at feasts, and the chief seats in the synagogues, And greetings in the markets, and to be called of men, Rabbi, Rabbi. But be not ye called Rabbi: for one is your Master, even Christ; and all ye are brethren. And call no man your father upon the earth: for one is your Father, which is in heaven. Neither be ye called masters: for one is your Master, even Christ. But he that is greatest among you shall be your servant. And whosoever shall exalt himself shall be abased; and he that shall humble himself shall be exalted.

It is by the grace of God that I avoid confrontation with these types of numbnuts who put much stock into religious toilet paper. I think it also has to do with the initial shock of the unbelievable. In other words, "Did I just hear what I thought I heard!?" Then, I find myself trying to give the benefit of the doubt until the action or similar actions are repeated. And yes, his actions were repeated which will have to be for another blog post.

As you can tell, I do not put any stock into religious toilet paper and have no bones with stating that toilet paper is worth more than the religious titles of men. In other words, my often interaction with toilet paper has more worth, value, and substance than the phone call with Snuffy will ever have. Jesus was not impressed by religious titles and neither am I. When people start using the religious title of "Servant," such as Servant Snuffy...then I will be impressed.

We ended up waiting out our time because God was preparing the way to move us out of the south and back to the north. I look back now and am amazed at the providence of God and his precise detail with what doors he closes and opens to direct our paths. I am just glad to be a passenger on the Bus.

RECRUITING

After my return from mobilization as a Drill Sergeant I began to research in more detail my active duty options. I just was not feeling peace about remaining in the area we were located and the chaplaincy was not a route I was feeling called to pursue. After much thought and prayer, I realized I had more ministry opportunity in the trenches with my fellow soldiers. After all I was with daily and for much of the day; whereas you might see a chaplain once a week and you really did not have the opportunity to get to know them on a personal level. This chapter consists of 12 years of my career and life and therefore is appropriately the longest chapter of this memoir.

I really enjoyed the Infantry and was considering reenlisting in the regular Army as an Infantryman. However, I would have to take a reduction in rank which I was not excited about doing considering I just made Sergeant First Class at the time. This is not an easy rank to come by and some retire without attaining it and most who do retire after twenty years do not surpass it. So I continued to research my other options.

One of those options I heard other soldiers speak of while I was on my active duty tour as a drill sergeant. This route would be to go Active Guard Reserve (AGR) which offers the same benefits as a Regular Army soldier. I was familiar with the recruiting path, but immediately ruled it out because of the horror stories I heard about recruiting in general. Little did I know that this is the path that the Lord would have me to travel. Even in this the Lord left a clear mark on the turn I should take once I arrived at the intersection of this decision. Actually he made it quite simple by as I could only turn in one direction due to the other option being road blocked.

My initial pursuit to go back on active duty was to be a NCOES instructor which I would have started out teaching new soon to be sergeants their Primary Leadership Development Course which is required to move on to the rank of sergeant. It is now called the Warrior Leader's Course. In order for me to take this position I would have had to take a reduction in rank which I was not so happy about doing. Nevertheless I was prepared to do so and had submitted my application for the job.

The Master Sergeant whose responsibility was to screen records for the position that I was applying for was excited to come across my packet. He stated that I was very well qualified for the job and that he wanted me in the position. So the process was initiated and it was time to wait for my reduction in rank orders back to Staff Sergeant and orders for the duty assignment.

Some time had passed since I heard anything about the status of my orders so I called Human Resources to inquire about the progress. The person I spoke with stated that my position was filled by someone else. After the initial shock I felt from what I just heard, I simply replied, "Do you have anything else available?" The person replied, "Yes we do, recruiting. Let me transfer you to the person who deals with this side of the house."

The Recruit the Recruiter representative was more than happy to speak with me and go over the opportunities that were available in the land of recruiting. After my questions were answered I was still apprehensive about the whole idea. I suppose I liked the idea that I would be able to retain my rank, so I asked when was the earliest I could report to recruiting school. He stated, "I am loading you a date right now for June" which happened to be only a couple months away. So as simple as that, I was now locked into the recruiting path.

I soon saw where God had a hand in all of it when I called the Master Sergeant who was looking to put me into one of his instructing positions. As soon as I explained that HRC said the position was filled by someone else he exclaimed with a few choice words that it was a mistake and that he could get it fixed. I asked him if he would be able to get it where I was able to keep my rank and he replied that he would not be able to. I then told the Master Sergeant that I would just stick with recruiting, and that is what I did even though I never thought I would actually go down that path.

Isaiah 55:8-9 For my thoughts are not your thoughts, neither are your ways my ways, saith the LORD. For as the heavens are higher than the earth, so are my ways higher than your ways, and my thoughts than your thoughts.

I initially was hoping that there was a recruiting position available at our location at the time mainly due to our financial obligation with our home and property. There were no openings at the time so I asked if there was anything available in my home state of Ohio. There were two openings available, one in Marietta and the other in Zanesville. As soon as I was given this information and I immediately began my research on both of the areas starting with what churches were in the area.

For some reason I liked the idea of Marietta a little better and called a church or so in the area. I was not able to get a hold of the pastors so I left a message and began to look at what was available in the Zanesville area. I did a search on on IFB church locator website and discovered that there was not much available. However, I did find one church and for some reason I did not realize that the word "Baptist" was not in the title. Later I discovered that the church was a "Bible" church which pretty much identified itself with the IFB movement.

I ended up talking with the associate pastor of this Bible church who was very friendly and knew how to answer all of my questions and avoid conversation that would turn me away. Based on our conversation that day and the perceived agreement that we had I called the Recruit the Recruiter team back and chose Zanesville as our first recruiting assignment.

So we immediately began to set things in motion for our move to Zanesville, Ohio. We put our property up for sale, even though it would not end up selling, and began to look for a new home at our soon to be new duty assignment. This also proved to be a challenge for us because we were looking for a house to purchase and there was not very many on the market at all that would fit the size of our family.

We found a good realtor named Dean who showed us quite a few homes that were available and none of them seemed to work for us. So we decided to drive around a desired neighborhood that we wanted to be located at and we ended up seeing a house that was for sale by owner. Due to our short house hunting visit we quickly set up an appointment with the owners to look at the house.

The house had three bedrooms and one full bathroom upstairs. The kitchen was outdated but had a nice little breakfast nook with a picture window that allowed us to view the decent size backyard for a city house. Even though it had its issues it seemed to be the best we were able to come upon in such a short period of time. We decided to put an offer on it which was soon accepted and the closing process began.

During our short house hunting visit we did our best to research the church we contacted and the school district. We were happy to leave our substandard church experience back in Georgia; however, the school district we liked. So we were hoping to find similar school conditions with and approved church experience back in the Buckeye State.

I should have realized that due to the church we were researching having a Christian school that they were going to expect us to attend their school. I was so naive to this that after the associate pastor gave me a tour of the church and school i asked him what he thought was the best school district in the area. He gave me a brief overview without giving too much detail with no doubt hoping that we would choose to send our kids to their Christian school.

After we had found our house, a church, and a suitable school district we headed back to South Carolina to prepare for our move. The plan was to move into our new home as soon as we closed on the house so that we would not have to make double payments. We were unable to sell our property so we decided to advertise a rent to own option which we were able to quickly find tenants which was a huge blessing and a curse at the same time. I can not stand the hassle of being a landlord which has proven to be a thorn in my side. However the whole experience has taught me a huge lesson when it comes to debt. It would be years later that I would vow to avoid debt at all possible for the rest of my life.

I was anxious and excited to leave the south to return to "Yankee" territory. I was hoping to find a new adventure awaiting us, regardless of the outcome I was just thankful to be returning to active duty eventually. As I look back now it was a huge step of faith and a big risk to make our move due to the fact that I was not guaranteed my position on active duty. Every recruiter had to have a background investigation completed prior to receiving active duty orders. Even though I did not have anything in my past to disqualify me it still took awhile to complete due to a backlog.

Nevertheless, we loaded our moving truck and vehicles and made our way back to the Buckeye State. There were not too many to say good-bye to since we moved church memberships and the church we left before our move probably was thinking more of good riddance, at least as far as the leadership went. My wife did make a couple close friends though which has been a blessing to our family. They stay in touch even unto this day. So our short time there was no doubt for a reason.

Thankfully we arrived safely to Zanesville, Ohio and our new home. We were blessed to have two families to assist us with unpacking our trucks. One of the men was a Navy veteran whom I would get to know a little better as the years went on. We never did get real close because of his loyalty to the church we initially attended together, even so somehow we were still able to maintain a mutual respect for each others calling.

As soon as we were all settled in I began to apply for some jobs so that we would have some additional resources while my background investigation was still pending. I ended up getting a job delivering pizza. I worked for about a month or so at the pizza shop until I was given an opportunity to go on a short active duty tour as a drill sergeant back in South Carolina. This worked out great for me! For one the pay was better, secondly my stay was flexible so that when I did receive orders for recruiting I could come back home and go to work.

The downsize to me going away has always been having to leave my family. Hence the life of a soldier, after all at the time the middle east wars were still young in respect to how long they would actually last so I felt that if I was in my previous military occupational skill of an Infantryman I would be deployed either way. The least I could do was support my brethren back here in the states as a drill sergeant and send them some well trained recruits which is not and was not an easy task.

I continued to take my job as a Drill Sergeant very seriously! I was probably one of the loudest and most strict drill sergeant at the time who did not let one infraction or detail go by my attention. We were trained to pay attention to detail in Drill Sergeant school especially when it came to drill and ceremony. We had to basically memorize verbatim each military drill movement which was a task that was quite overwhelming but somehow by the grace of God I managed to do it. It really showed me what we can with our minds with a little determination.

Bosom of a Stranger

When I was a Drill Sergeant I had a Sergeant Major who briefed us as new Drills and said something like, "If you want to commit a sexual impropriety with one of the trainees, I want to personally meet that soldier. Why? Because that soldier is worth over $500k, which is about what your retirement in the toilet equates to."

Proverbs 5:18-20 Let thy fountain be blessed: and rejoice with the wife of thy youth. Let her be as the loving hind and pleasant roe; let her breasts satisfy thee at all times; and be thou ravished always with her love. And why wilt thou, my son, be ravished with a strange woman, and embrace the bosom of a stranger?

The national headlines have been inundated with those who have been "ravished with strange women" and have embraced their bosom's mostly without consent. Even if it is with consent such as from a prostitute, the bosom is still from a stranger. A stranger that is foreign to the nuclear family and can haunt it throughout a lifetime.

Even today in the national spotlight there is a judge who is campaigning for the senate who has repeatedly denied the molestation of multiple women, some who happened to be in their teens. I mention this example because he states that the accusations are an assault upon his Christianity.

Based on the facts that have been presented I do not see where the testimonies of the accusers are not credible. Furthermore, I have seen news clips where this judge denies these accusations in houses of worship without speaking or appearing credible in his denial which brings me to the remainder of the text in Proverbs 5.

Proverbs 5:21-23 For the ways of man are before the eyes of the LORD, and he pondereth all his goings. His own iniquities shall take the wicked himself, and he shall be holden with the cords of his sins. He shall die without instruction; and in the greatness of his folly he shall go astray.

If this judge is spinning a web of deceit, he will be caught in it one way or the other. God knows our ways, everyone of them, and the balance of his thoughts weighs our actions. What infuriates me the most about this whole scenario is when there are attempts to use Christianity as a shield to protect deceit.

In the midst of all this turmoil, the judge has a wife. You want to know what keeps me from strange women? My wife. Why? Because I love her and would never want to break her heart. The moment I allow my lust to fall into the hands of a strange woman is a moment that sacks decades of love and trust.

Let's consider this in monetary terms and say that my wife and I have saved, saved, and saved some more over the years to the point our bank account has reached a nice sum. Then one day a strange lady walks down the street, winks and eye, and I decide to empty our account into the stranger's hands. Where does this leave us? Broke. On the flip side, such as with the allegations against the judge, he is the perpetrator robbing the bank of love and trust that belongs to the victim. In these cases it will be years if not decades to regain that which is lost for them too.

Not the perpetrating stranger though, the stranger walks away with something that never belonged to her or him. Sin becomes a trophy for the stranger. Think about it, if we are willing to empty our life savings for a lustful moment with a stranger, betray all of the love and trust that has been built up for decades, what a trophy this must be in the eyes of the stranger. The stranger says, "I must be somebody for a stranger to give up all that they have to be with me." Consensual or even worse non-consensual fulfilled lust with strangers, those other than a spouse, always leads us into great folly....leading us astray.

Provide the Strength

My new job began to provide the strength for our Army, which was not an easy task at all. We had just commenced the Iraq war a year and a half prior to my start date, so the public was not exactly jumping at the opportunity to serve. There was a good spike in recruiting after 9/11 as a result of the rise of patriotic retribution, but by the time I started recruiting people were already becoming weary and apathetic to the ongoing war saga in the Middle East.

Many recruiters allowed this same type of attitude to carry over into their work also which affected their productivity. I was new and energized and wanted to do well at my new job. I felt it was my duty to produce; plus I wanted to be an example for the faith, not an excuse of why someone would not choose to follow Christ. God no doubt blessed me with a determined and focused work ethic. I just may have tapped into it more than I should by working more hours than I was required to and neglecting the more important aspects of my life such as faith and family.

As I look back, I feel that as though those days were darker not realizing that God was developing the groundwork for a future ministry. I know my calling and felt that it would not blossom until my retirement from the Army. I am reminded of the encouraging fact that the Lord is continually at work in our lives and always has a plan. We just need to continue pushing forward. The pushing forward reminds me of the many foot patrols I have been on in my military career, especially those that have been through wooded terrain. We have had to move over and through just about every landscape there is to reach our objective. I especially disliked moving through water on cold days and having to bust through thick vegetation we called "wait-a-minute-vines".

This reminds me of the Special Forces training I attended which provided the best land navigation training and course in the world. I happened to not be far on the course when I saw a small little bridge that was between a pond and a large area of "wait-a-minute-vines". The instructors specifically stated that we were not to use the bridges on the course. However, I noticed that there was a small clear path on either side of the bridge, so I decided to use one of the small paths.

When I was halfway through to the other side I heard a loud whisper yell "Hey! Candidate! Where are you going?". I immediately replied that I was not "on" the bridge and he cut me off and told me to go the way of the water or go through the brush. I quietly turned around and started to move around the pond carefully so that I would not lose my navigational bearing. I have learned that life is much like this experience. I suppose all of us are looking for those convenient bridges that are placed right in front of our face. However this is obviously not the will or way of God. He wants us to bust through the brush of life and allow the cold water on cold days to bring us back to reality.

I feel that this time in my life during the initial years of recruiting I was busting through "wait-a-minute-vines" doing my best to stay on course. I also needed to walk through a few cold ponds to shock me into reality concerning the state of the local church because as I look back now I was allowing myself to be naive to the inefficiencies and traps that were created for power and control without genuine concern for the will of God for individual lives.

It did not take me long to figure out that the church we decided to attend during this initial period of recruiting was lifeless. As for the few strands of life that existed, those were the ones that my family was attracted to. Concerning the others, it was quite obvious that they did not want anything to do with us once they realize that we would not immediately conform to their model of Christianity. It just so happens that a huge part of that model is their Christian school. So when they found out that our children were going to the public school there is no doubt in my mind we were marked as a divisive threat.

I have learned since that the reason there is such a struggle with elementary, secondary, and Bible campus education is that in order to maintain the huge monetary structures and staffs you have to have willing people to fund them. Ever since my salvation I have been blindly funding these efforts through my tithes and offerings. The assumption has always been that the funds were in the care of men of God who would prayerfully distribute the giving in accordance with the will of God and fund his kingdom. The sad reality is that this in many cases in not so at all. The funds are distributed without prayer or God's kingdom in mind at all. The main concern is how do we keep these structures and staffs maintained.

I am not saying that no good at all comes out of organizations such as these. Think about it though, there are moments of good that flow out of the most vile of human beings. So a few scraps of good will towards men does not constitute for fulfilling the will of God. On the other hand, I would be remiss if I did not mention the sparks of hope that have existed in these types of churches we have attended. We have met quite a few genuine people do their best to accomplish the will of God for their lives. Although, for whatever reason, many of the same choose to remain restricted to the confines of their kingdoms.

I have tried over the years to give all who profess Christ and the ministries that we have been a part of the benefit of the doubt concerning their position with Christ. Afterall, it is my hope that others would do the same for me and my family. We are far from perfect that is for sure and I do not expect the people of the church as a whole to be perfect. However when the ministry's light is dying out, I do not feel as though we should be silent about it. We should be discussing what we need to do in order to get back on track even if that means branching out or starting over.

With starting over in mind we decided to look for another church and ended up visiting a church that was about a fifteen minute drive away. I called the pastor and he agreed to come to our house so we could discuss details concerning the church and where they stood on various areas of the faith. I was upfront with the pastor on exactly where we stood on issues such as schooling, Bible translations, and music. We would not be there too long before we realized that he was not as open and honest with us.

Looking back it is clear to me the reason why this pastor was less than forthcoming is the same reason why most who are in his shoes respond in the same manner. The reason mostly has to do with paying the bills. In order to pay the bills you have to have a source of income and for the professional preacher that source of income tends to be from the tithers.

When I first became a Christian this was a sore spot for me when it came to the tithe. Hower after being educated during my discipleship there was a specific class that dealt with the topic in a thorough manner with the Old Testament standard of the tenth or 10% of income. At first 10% was very hard for me to swallow, but when it was presented in the light of the fact that God owns 100% and is only asking for us to contribute a minimum of 10% by faith I could then see the significance pertaining to the overall exercise of faith.

A Soldier's Progress

Hebrews 7:2a To whom also Abraham gave a tenth part of all...

Based on our initial conversation with the pastor of the new church we were looking at he could easily come to the conclusion that we were more than likely tithers. Obviously the more tithers a church has the more stable those who depend upon the giving are going to be at least financially anyways. This is where the fine line of personal and church kingdom building versus Kingdom of God building. When focusing on the Kingdom of God the resources are already provided for the work that God has called each of to do. No need to worry, but this the pastor did. I must have a little empathy though and I do. His family consisted of nine children at the time.

Those who serve in the ministry in a full time capacity I respect, however I also respect the fact that one must be ready at all times to get a job if need be. After All, this is not exactly a bad situation to be in and God happens to orchestrate this scenario all the time. I know this for a fact because these are the conditions he has created for my life this far.

Anyways this same pastor faced a trial in his life and ministry when the church collaborated to fire him. After a few months of attending the church I could see why due to his laziness and pity party he showed forth so that others would feel sorry for him and his family and give them handouts. We felt sorry for them as well and wanted to be a blessing on a couple of occasions which looking back we now regret in some ways because of the response we received.

The culture of Independent Baptist churches I do believe created the attitude of the honor handout mentality. In other words, many men and women who are in a position of authority within these churches feel that handouts are expected for the "man and woman of God", therefore no thanks is required. I found this attitude rather repulsive even though we gave unto the Lord anyways.

The sad part is that this pattern of unthankfulness was being passed on to their children. Anytime there was a church or group gathering with the family the pastor's kids would swarm the food line like rabid dogs with little supervision at all. Again, I do believe that the family felt this was owed to them. I would later sit down with the pastor when we decided to leave the church for good to pursue the new direction God was leading us towards and confront him about this unthankfulness. I told him even though it was an irritation and something they needed to work on that it was not the reason we were leaving the church.

We decided to leave this church after a series of events which caused me to see that God had a mission for my family that in all reality I was running from or to ignorant to realize that all I had to do was step out on faith to begin the new leg of my spiritual journey. Despite my ignorance and lack of faith God was faithful as he always is and painted me in a corner with the negative events I was experiencing at the churches we attended.

The straw breaker ended up occurring as the result of a special speaker that ended up being invited to preach at the same church of the pastor I have just described. The older gentleman preached outside under the pavilion while I was tending to my youngest son Larry as he ran around in the field. All was well until the man began to preach about how wicked it was for Christians to send their children to public school. There is not a doubt in my mind that this was a request of the pastor, although I cannot say for sure. Nevertheless, it was enough for me to start listening to what God would really have me to do.

SPC. Kyle P. Norris

"On 23 May 2008, Army Spc. Kyle P. Norris; assigned to the 3rd Battalion, 7th Infantry Regiment, 4th Brigade Combat Team, 101st Airborne Division Air Assault, Ft. Campbell, KY, died of wounds sustained when his vehicle encountered an improvised explosive device."[6]

John 15:13 Greater love hath no man than this, that a man lay down his life for his friends.

SPC. Norris is the first fallen soldier our recruiting station enlisted during my recruiting tour. I remember Norris very well because of how long his enlistment process was drawn out. He needed two or three waivers to get in and on top of it all he had to gain weight. After about a year or so along with a highly determined applicant, Norris finally was on his way to become a United States Army soldier.

Norris successfully completed his Initial Entry Training and

[6] Military Times https://thefallen.militarytimes.com/army-spc-kyle-p-norris/3551094

when he returned home on his first visits was back to the recruiting station. All of the recruiters to include myself were very proud of all the hard work he put in to obtain his dream. Norris would continue to stay in contact with us on MySpace at the time and for the remainder of his service until one day we received the news that SPC. Norris had been Killed In Action.

This was devastating news to our recruiting station. Immediately upon receiving the news I made contact with Ms. Norris, Kyle's Mother, and gave our condolences. Ms. Norris happens to be a great Christian and upon Kyle's death a new Gold Star Mother. Over the years we continue to stay in touch with Ms. Norris and we consider her family to be part of ours.

The most comforting news that we received concerning Kyle after his death was that he too was a Christian. I was given a photocopy of his Bible that bears witness to the spiritual condition of SPC. Kyle P. Norris. Written under the "Occasions to Remember" section Kyle writes, "Got saved on Aug. 4, 2004. Started reading the Bible on May 24, 2005 from the beginning. Made it in the Army on Dec. 24, 2005."

THE SOLDIER'S SANCTUARY

The church gathering that caused the major shift in my spiritual journey met at the end of May in 2008 around the same time we received the news concerning SPC. Norris. The week or so after the meeting the Lord gave me my mission and I accepted even though I did not know exactly how I was to accomplish it. All I knew was what I experienced in the Baptist churches I attended and the little I learned in a Baptist Bible college within the previous fifteen years.

The first step I took was to call my very good friend Rick (Wise) who was one of my soldiers who had and still has an awesome attitude and a great work ethic. I called him and told him bluntly that it was a long story but the Lord was leading me to start a church. I told him, "I only have one question Wise, are you in?". He quickly replied, "I am in!". Bam! That is all it took for the Soldier's Baptist Church to be born.

The name is very ironic considering that many in Baptist church where I attended when the Lord saved me thought the Army would hinder my faith. I am still amazed until this day that many of the same do not see that the military is an awesome mission field with great need. I did not know this when God called me to join the Army either. I seemed to always think that I would eventually be in the "full time" ministry after my service in the Army was completed, not realizing that God had placed me in his full time service from day one.

All I knew up to the point of our church plant was the

Baptist way of life and at the time I felt it necessary to define our church as a Baptist church considering all of the various theological stands that exists within the Christian society. Not only did we include the name Baptist in our title, we patterned our ministry after the denomination's model which I now know is not incomplete accordance with the Biblical model. I will speak more about how our church model morphed later.

When the Lord saved me there was not a host of people lined up to encourage me to discover the will of God for my life and accomplish it. I really do believe that whether many Christians would like to admit it or not, they are often afraid to do so because their laborers may be called to go out and start a work which would take away from their own. This too was evident with the beginning of the Soldier's Baptist Church. There was no one but our initial members who went out of the way to encourage us or support us as we began our work for the Lord.

On June 1, 2008 we met at our house for our first church service. Those in attendance consisted of my wife, children, and Rick who was unmarried at the time. I do not remember the exact details of that service, all I know is that we prayed, sang, preached the Word, and fellowshipped. A huge weight had been lifted from my heart and soul as we worshipped together that day due to the step of faith that was taken along with the defiance of the religious and traditional status quo.

Within the next few weeks are attendance began to grow. I ended up calling a young man I had met while recruiting at our local college who has spina bifida. We would eventually give him the name of Gripper due to his strong hand grip developed by his mode of predominant travel which are his hands and arms. When I got a hold of him I approached him much in the same manner as I did Rick and Gripper stated, "I am in!". Gripper is a great supporter of the American soldier and if he had the opportunity to enlist today he absolutely would. Instead he has been serving with a volunteer civil war reenactment unit and continues to show his support for our military by the means of social media regularly.

Our next recruit Jim I had initially met when he came into the recruiting office to look at the possibility of going into the Army Reserves. We did all of his paperwork and back then it took months for the command to approve a rank determination waiver. Five or six months passed and Jim in his frustration decided to join the National Guard instead. The day that our waiver came through for Jim I call him with the good news. He stated, "Sorry, I am signing papers with the Guard right now!"

Not long after this Jim opened a barber shop in our town and I started to get haircuts at his shop. Even though Jim was a little "crass" as one recruiter who worked for me stated, I enjoyed his fellowship as we talked about our experiences in the Army. We laughed together about the different leaders we had and their style of leadership. We also laughed at how we led our own soldiers. Initially we didn't talk much about the Lord. I was waiting for that opportunity and door to open at the right moment.

Well it seemed that that right moment was around a campfire during a camping trip that I was not in attendance at. Rick was though, I had introduced him to Jim's barber shop and they struck a friendship as well. While sitting around the fire Rick brought up the discussion concerning our new church by stating "Andy and I started a church". This statement caught Jim off guard as he practically spit out his beer and said "a church!".

Jim immediately was brought back to a few years prior when his wife was having complications during the birth of their son. The situation was not looking good at all for either of them. Jim felt inclined due to his previous church attendance as a teenager to rush down to the hospital chapel and get on his knees to seek God for the purpose of sparing his wife and child. At that time he told the Lord if he did that he would start going back to church. Jim felt that Rick's declaration was now that time to fulfill his promise.

Within a couple of weeks after Jim and his family started attending Sunday services at our home a fellow recruiter name James and his wife also started attending. We were not initially trying to recruit James because he was attending the church we had just left. My intent was to continue support and respect for the church to include not influencing any of the members to leave their church.

Quite a few months past before the door opened to share the Gospel with James and his wife. Our conversation up until that point mostly consisted of recruiting and UFC mixed martial arts. James knew I was a Christian and one day we were driving somewhere to conduct our recruiting duties for the Army and James said that he was ready to look further into the Christian way of life. Those were the only words needed to open the floodgates concerning our Christian conversation.

I told James my testimony and ended with "James, think about all that I have told you concerning Jesus Christ and his salvation. If you feel that you are ready to cross that bridge I will schedule another meeting with you and your wife to pray with you and discuss salvation with your wife as well if you would like me to do so". He thought that was a great plan and sure enough a few days later, James and his wife accepted Jesus Christ as their Savior.

Finally concerning the charter members of the Soldier's Baptist Church we ended up having another one of our fellow recruiters attend whose name is Brad. He is a brother in Christ who had been out of church for quite a long while. He was glad to see his brothers in arms and brothers in Christ leading services.

There were six men, including myself, who became the charter members of the Soldier's Baptist Church. RIght away I developed and patterned our constitution and how we were to conduct business as a church. Our members agreed to conduct an ordination service appointing me as their pastor. I was honored to have the signatures of my fellow five charter members Rick, Jim, James, Gripper, and Brad on my ordination certificate. I would not trade those signatures for the most profound and famous clergyman in the world.

We ended up establishing a church bank account to account for the giving of our members after I found out that all we needed was a tax identification number. I also learned that we as a church were not required to apply for non-profit status due to being a church. I am glad that our laws are structured in this manner. I even read on the IRS website where a writer question why churches sought for non-profit status in the first place. Managing the giving was not as time consuming as I thought it would be, I ended up using a live Google document so each member could login and track their giving and the total giving of the church along with expenses.

The first year of our ministry was explosive! We were using our home's large bath tub to baptize many that accepted Jesus Christ as their Savior. As I type I do not have the exact number, but there were over 40 who were saved and baptized within that year. Those who were not baptized in our tub were baptized in the local river on days the weather permitted.

Upon the baptism of each new Christian they became members of the Soldier's Baptist Church and each were given a baptismal certificate. We were careful to explain the seriousness and significance of baptism prior to scheduling a date for each baptismal service. By the way no one who has been saved while attending our services has refused baptism. I mention this because of those who teach you must be baptized in order to be saved. My question is "Who refuses to be baptized that is genuinely saved?" If a true believer has the opportunity to get baptized they will. However there are those who have not had the opportunity such as the thief on the cross.

So as a church we set out to fulfill the Great Commission to see people surrender to our Lord and Savior Jesus Christ, get baptized and carry out the meaning of baptism which is to be dead to our old lives and live the new life that God birthed us according to his perfect will. Also in order to assist in this effort we developed a discipleship schedule that included Sunday School and weekly meetings for the men and women.

Our men created a core group called the Junto based on Benjamin Franklin's premise of an inner circle of men who had an unbreakable friendship and loyalty to one another creating an ideal condition for the ability to share ideas to promote our cause and better our lives for the glory of God. The ladies created something similar which they called the Yada Yada ladies based on a book that my wife read.

These core groups were central to the initial growth of our church. Each relationship within the group was built upon trust, friendship, and our mutual faith. The light that shone forth to others attracted family members, friends, and acquaintances to attend our services. Without these core principles I do not believe we would have been able to mobilize an all volunteer force to be able to sustain our growth.

We were forced to learn as things occurred even though I personally have had many years of church and Bible education to draw from. We learned from each experience by researching the various avenues of approach for any issue or question we were faced with. Communication with the team was critical for these moments to discuss, collaborate, formulate a plan, and then to execute the plan. I was blessed to have the support of my brothers for all decisive actions I took as I felt the Lord leading.

As a result of our fast growth I feel that now looking back I was attempting to meet the demands of the existing church model I grew up in and knew. Much of this model consisted of success being viewed in numbers. The more numbers you experience as a church, the more you are blessed and experiencing the hand of God and work. I have learned since that this far from the truth.

We eventually began to add those to the church that more than likely should not have been added to the church. This caused me to have to put out a few fires that may have never needed to be started if I would have approached our church operations in a more Biblical manner I think we could have avoided some of the few issues we experienced during our growing pains.

Some of the ladies attending our church were starting to gossip and create a little havoc. As I try to recall the details of the situations they escape me; however, the resolution does not. I have come to the conclusion that in any situation to include church relationships that communication is key. Face to face communication that is. So I coordinated a series of face to face meetings to resolve the issues we face at the time.

One of those meetings I remember vividly was at Jim's barber shop. As we sat there, I opened up the conversation with the reason we were all gathered and paused. During the pause Jim shouted "If you do not like it here, LEAVE!!!!" In a way I felt bad for the men we were trying to confront, but at the same time Jim's blunt outburst was welcomed at fulfilled the intent of the seriousness of our mission and friendship.

We lost a few families after these meetings and as sorry as I am to see them leave, I started to learn that numbers and premature memberships can cause a whole lot of heartache and actually hinder the overall mission. A good indicator of someone just filling a number and not part of the mission is when they do not have no desire to be discipled. A valuable team member wants to learn about the team's doctrine, operating procedures, and culture. If not, as Jim stated...let them leave and as I have stated many times, MOVE OUT!

Our growth moved us out of my house into a rented building that accommodated 50 people to the American

Legion banquet hall which was able to facilitate at least 200. The attitude that I have nothing to lose and nothing to gain in the ministry began to take quick roots in my soul and revolutionized how I dealt with newcomers to our church. Once we had a family that attended one Sunday morning who acted like we should roll out the red carpet and wait on them hand and foot. When I explained to them that we were an all volunteer church where everyone pitched in they replied, "Oh, we can't do that, we need a break and just need to be fed". Well, little did they know that part of the TSS spiritual diet included volunteer work. Needless to say, that family did not stick around very long.

One of the greatest advantages of operating a church with little overhead is the ability to utilize church discipline without fear of monetary loss. Too many preachers I have come to know over the years feared this scenario very much. A wealthy family would be a part of the church and they were deathly afraid to offend the family knowing they could potentially leave and put a huge dent in the church budget. Well, all I have to say to these types of folks who think they have a financial anchor within our ministry is MOVE OUT!

Our military core group of men understood what work ethic and teamwork was all about. This is why I am glad called me to enlist in the Army. I needed the training that is provided in the military to help mold me and shape me into the person I am today. I have learned what sacrifice, honor, duty, and commitment are. These things along with passion and camaraderie are the ingredients that fueled our drive to accomplish the mission that God had set before us in our small nonmilitary city.

My initial approach and vision was patterned after what I knew and the way I was trained. Find as many as we could who were willing to recite the sinner's prayer of salvation and encourage them to be baptized. Then upon their baptism they would be added to the church as members where they then would be encouraged to attend weekly meetings which were held on Sunday's and bi-monthly for the men and women's midweek small groups studies and fellowships.

We were comfortable with our Sunday gatherings where we all helped with the setup and teardown of our meeting locations. Our services consisted of a Sunday School hour where we covered mostly discipleship topics and a worship hour that included prayer, Bible reading, praises, singing, and preaching. Most all services were ended with some sort of invitation for nonbelievers to come forward and surrender their lives to Christ.

I am humbled to be able to report that the Lord did a miraculous and wonderful work in many of the lives of those who attended our church. We were glad to see many surrender their faith to the Lord Jesus Christ and be baptized. I thought that many of our fellow brothers in Christ and local ministries would feel the same. Well, they did not.

One day I was invited to participate in a local Christian radio program and was asked by the host, "What is the name of your soldier thingy you have going on?" I could tell that he was not all that excited about another ministry being a softball throw away from his, but yet he went through the motions of supporting the brotherhood and had me on his show where he mainly focused on our Army mission versus our spiritual one. This same "minister" would eventually run off on his wife with another woman.

This type of attitude was not uncommon and much of it I am convinced is a result of the turf wars that exist within in Christianity. The wars are a constant struggle over dwindling resources which happen to be people and their giving. Most of the religious gestapo in the area completely ignored our ministry. However we were able to reach out and touch bases with one other like minded ministry. I also happen to share the same first name with the former pastor. He is longer with the church which is another story I am sure.

Initially, we decided to meet at a hole in the wall diner and we discussed what God was doing in our churches and the challenges we faced. I stressed to him the importance of core loyalty amongst the men and how I believed God used our genuine friendship with one another for his honor and glory. Andy would later help us load up our moving truck and see us off to New York. He told me then how fed up he was with Independent Fundamental Baptists and I told him I would rather shovel human waste than to be ensnared by those types of puppet strings.

LOVE NEW YORK?

The time had come for us to move on to New York. I had
received an email from command that stated I had not done a
cost move since 2004 and that I need to pick from the places
they were offering or they were going to pick a place for me.
Initially I chose an assignment in Salina, Kansas. I called the
First Sergeant responsible for the Salina recruiting station and
told him a little about who I was and he basically replied, "I
do not care who you are or where you came from! You will be
judged based on your performance when you get here. Let's
just hope we don't have to take you to shredder hill." Well, this
attitude and response did not fly very well with me at all.

As a result of this uncalled for and unwarranted response I
immediately did not feel well at all about going to Salina.
However before I decided to see what I could do about getting
rerouted I gave it some time and began to research the area.
One of the areas I researched was the church scene. I found a
church that was looking for a pastor and decided to give them
a call.

I ended up speaking with a lady from the church and talked
to her for a while and told her all that the Lord had done up to
that point with the ministry of The Soldier's Sanctuary. She
replied many times for me to submit a "resume" and I kept
replying that I was not applying for a job which is the same
way I feel today when it comes to ministry positions. I am not
concerned with applying to become a hireling, I am concerned
with accomplishing the will of God for my life period.

A Soldier's Progress

John 10:12 But he that is an hireling, and not the shepherd, whose own the sheep are not, seeth the wolf coming, and leaveth the sheep, and fleeth: and the wolf catcheth them, and scattereth the sheep.

The Lord quickly closed the door to Salina though when I emailed headquarters and asked to take a leadership position instead. At first they replied that I had not had the proper schooling for the positions and then I explained how the command felt it proper to have me lead in these positions for years knowing that I had not been to the required school. After this point was made the command scheduled me for the next leader course and I received follow on orders to New York.

It was sad leaving Zanesville and all of the relationships that the Lord allowed us to be a part of . At least with all of the negatives that are a result of social media the one positive is that we have been able to keep up with many of these same people. Nevertheless it was still hard. My closest of friends Rick and Jim stood by my side to the very end as they helped us load our moving truck and waved us off. When we arrived in New York we moved into military housing that consisted of mostly Marines due to a Marine post being nearby at the Stewart Air Base which was actually within walking distance. I didn't care so much for the duplex housing set up, but at the same time I could not complain because we had plenty of room with access to a community gym and pool.

One of the first task we set to accomplish was our place of worship. In the same building as the community gym there was a perfect place for us to be able to conduct Sunday Services. We had a few services there and I believe we had a child attend but besides that it was just our family even though we did our best to spread the word. With all of the crackpots in the world I am not ignorant to the fact that people are not just going to fall in line overnight when it comes to participating with those who preach and teach the Bible. So, I started to reach out to the existing Christian community and let them know what we were doing and what our purpose was.

One of the first people that I spoke with from the local Christian community was a Chaplain from West Point. I explained to him what we were doing and how I wanted to be able to plug my wife into a women's ministry. He told me about the PWOC ladies ministry which stands for Protestant Women of the Chapel. Soon after Lin was plugged into the great work they had on post. The amazing part about the PWOC connection was the fact that there was no Chaplain or Christian support connected with our military housing. PWOC provided this connection and my wife had the awesome opportunity to lead the overall effort. It was not long at all before my missionary wife was in action inviting all of the ladies she could in our community to attend PWOC with her. A number of ladies would soon attend.

One of the ladies that began attending PWOC with Lin was Jenny who was married to a Marine. They immediately connected in a special way and are very good friends till this day. Together they would reach out to the rest of our military community and many other ladies began to attend the weekly PWOC meetings as the lives were transformed for the glory of

God.

Lin wanted her ministry to extend beyond the ladies in the community and reach the children as well so she started a weekly girls group called "God's Girls". It wasn't long at all before a couple of handfuls of girls began attending. Each week the Lin and the ladies who assisted would prepare a craft and lesson that captured the attention of the girls to the point where they began inviting their friends Jenny kept God's Girls going even after we were reassigned due to a promotion I received.

While Lin and the ladies were reaching out to each other and the girls I was reaching out to their husbands and fathers. One of them men that I had the opportunity to lead to the Lord shared the same first name with me. He and another soldier attended a Bible Study at my house where soon after he called upon the Lord for salvation. We were honored to present his family with a Bible and see him get plugged into church where his family became active.

We were not in the New Windsor area for long. As usual recruiting was highly stressful with a burden of numbers to meet monthly. Often in the New Windsor recruiting office I would find myself on my knees with the door closed in prayer asking God to help us meet the numbers we were missioned to achieve. Thankfully I would often find myself back on my knees in praise for God blessing our work.

One day I found myself praising God on my knees in the same office for something else which happened to be a selection for promotion to Master Sergeant E-8. This selection was no small feat and had to be ordained by God due to the highly competitive nature of the selection process. There were only a handful out of hundreds of qualified soldiers selected for this promotion and I happened to be one of them. This promotion would move us again.

A year after we arrived to New Windsor we received orders to go to Albany, New York where I would serve as an operations supervisor. As soon as we arrived and before we could even finish packing I was busy at work. However, it was a different type of work and the plus side was that I could walk to work. We ended up getting housing on the Watervliet Arsenal which is just about one of the oldest arsenal's on the American books. There were only about thirteen or so housing units and we were able to get a four bedroom house which was just one house in a big house of three. The house was an 1800's build that was converted into three units. Out of the three we like ours the best. It was no doubt the biggest house that we will most likely every live in on this side of Heaven that is for sure.

Limbo

Have you ever felt like you were in a spiritual limbo or a waiting cell? Well, I have and Upstate New York was that place. This was my last duty station and a day probably did not go by that I was not counting down to retirement. By the way, there are a few who are in a waiting cell, waiting for me to finish this memoir which highlights my Christian journey for the past 25 years- 22 of those years in the Army.

A Soldier's Progress

Psalms 130:5 I wait for the LORD, my soul doth wait, and in his word do I hope.

There are high walls around the perimeter of the arsenal that I found myself walking and running the interior of for many of the days we lived there. The laps around the arsenal were a time for prayer and thought processing. What was my purpose in New York for this second and last assignment in a state I never even visited? Yes, I know what my job and daily task were as a leader within a Recruiting Battalion. But, what was my real task? This has been my thought process these 25 years as a Christian. Whether on a deployment, field exercises, training school, new duty assignment, or wherever I was to experience a new environment with a new group of people I would begin to seek my purpose at the new location and ask, "How LORD am I to present the Gospel to these people?"

As you may have noticed from early experiences with this thought process I was a little more impatient, not so willing to "wait for the LORD." Many times I would roll into a new location and group of people with a spiritual double barrel shotgun and tell as many as I could my testimony of how I became a Christian and the Gospel message. As time passed, I learned that sometimes we have to wait.

This waiting process and time is essential when dealing with and interacting with others. I have no idea where the thought originated; but, "people do not care how much you know until they know how much you care" has resonated with me for years and I have seen this behavior and response over and over. People also want to know that you live up to what you preach. I may have not always lived up to what I preach, but I do try to be transparent about my failures which, in essence, is part of living up to what we preach.

Anyways, this process takes time. I have also realized that it is not my responsibility to "save" everyone around me and that there is a cost involved. Contrary to the Commercial Christianity belief of fame and popularity, I was not famous or even close to popular throughout my Army career for taking a stand for the faith. I experienced this once again rather quickly while assigned to my last Recruiting Battalion.

As a senior non-commissioned officer I worked very closely with the most senior non-commissioned officer who worked side by side with the battalion commander. Once this man found out that I was "religious," he kept his distance which did not make the most conducive office conditions. All I could do was wait and remind myself that God had us there for a reason and purpose. God knew exactly those people who we would have the opportunity to impact in a place I felt was like limbo.

Slow Death of a Church

When we arrived at Upstate, New York there were no physical lepers to cleanse, and I am not fully aware of what devils if any were cast out. All I know is that we were looking to see as many as we could raise from the spiritual dead unto spiritual life by means of salvation and if a few devils were cast out at the same time even if we were unaware that was great too! Our mindset then, as it is still today, was to freely preach the Gospel as we had freely received it.

Matthew 10:7-11 And as ye go, preach, saying, The kingdom of heaven is at hand. Heal the sick, cleanse the lepers, raise the dead, cast out devils: freely ye have received, freely give. Provide neither gold, nor silver, nor brass in your purses, Nor scrip for your journey, neither two coats, neither shoes, nor yet staves: for the workman is worthy of his meat. And into whatsoever city or town ye shall enter, enquire who in it is worthy; and there abide till ye go thence.

My wife found an old historic church outside the gate of the arsenal in a very small town. They had a thrift store and my wife loves to go thrift store shopping. I am not sure what she enjoys more- the shopping or the talking. Anyways, during her conversation she made it known that I preach. After a few more visits and conversations the church invited me to fill in for their pastor and preach on several Sundays. This was great! We were able to meet at an actual church for once. We have met at parks, houses, veterans organizations, rented office space, and finally an actual church.

After each Sunday service, one of the older board members would present me with a check and with gratitude I gladly accepted and then donated it back to the church each time. This was the best way to let the church know that they were being a blessing in return, I did not want to outright deny them of this blessing. So, I just immediately returned the blessing because the church desperately needed the funding and I did not.

I was shocked by how many beautiful historic churches struggled to stay alive in the Albany area. Christianity seemingly was dying a slow death and this church was under the same spell. For those who actually showed up to church I wondered if they even had a clue. One Sunday, I was invited to this same historic church to preach I preached a forgiveness message called "Seventy Times Seven." After the end of the message I gave an invitation to the congregation to come forward if they did not know Jesus as their Savior. I was absolutely amazed to see over half of those that attended come forward to accept the LORD into their lives.

After the service, one of the ladies came up to me and said, "You do not know how much we needed that message! All we do is fight around here and there is a lot of bitterness." Another lady at the thrift store will bear her heart with my wife on the same condition of the church and how they struggled to maintain the church's physical existence. This was very concerning to me knowing that at the same time their spiritual existence was being overlooked.

Isaiah 62:10   Go through, go through the gates; prepare ye the way of the people; cast up, cast up the highway; gather out the stones; lift up a standard for the people.

Not long after the "Seventy Seven" Sunday service at the historic church we saw the potential to not only help the church spiritually, but financially as well. I decided to write up an offer to the church board seeking rental space in the church for an hour or so for the purpose of conducting a Sunday service for The Soldier's Sanctuary. We had already made contact with many on our post and the church was already renting space and time to other organizations in the area, such as a theater outfit, to help support the church financially. After a meeting or two, some internal bickering, and a few weeks the answer to our offer arrived- NO.

This response did not hinder our outreach and God only knows, we may have been saved a huge headache from the result of the church's decision. Instead of having a solid fixed location such as the church, we went to what doesn't take a committee to approve. Bible studies and small groups seem to always be an available option with no red tape. I would see this red tape over and over again throughout my life in the church that is for sure.

Where do you go when there is a gaggle of red tape tripping you everywhere you step? Outside of the wire that is where you go and that is where we went. We did not need a physical location within the wire to meet people, share the Gospel, and meet other Christians. The church came to us, we did not have to go to it. My wife's snack bar became the church as she took time to get to know her customers which led into a women's Bible study. We were able to meet our neighbors, which added to the ladies Bible study and started a men's Bible study.

Our work outside the wire did not stop there either, we were able to me many other Christians on and off the arsenal who did not seek our fellowship to recruit us for their church. They just wanted another Christian to value them and appreciate them without feeling they were just another "nickel and nose," as one writer has stated it. One of these people we met was part of the law enforcement on the arsenal and a retired Special Forces soldier. My wife first met him while serving him at her snack bar. She shared our mission with the guard and thought it would be great if he could meet me one day.

One day I was getting ready to run a lap around the arsenal and a patrol car drove by. I noticed it was the guard my wife met at her snack bar. He stopped and we began to chat. I briefly shared with him my testimony and our mission with The Soldier's Sanctuary and while doing so his eyes watered up with tears. We ended our discussion with a plan to meet for fellowship. Weeks later, D7M and I would find ourselves in a McDonald's drinking coffee, sharing our testimonies, and experiencing church outside of the wire. We are friends still today and keep in contact even as he presently continues to do great things for our country overseas working with our military.

Ground of Respect

Exodus 2:25...and God had respect unto them.

D7M would not be the only Christian I would meet face to face outside of the wire. There is something about a face to face encounter that is essential for relationship building. Why else would people fly all over the world and drive thousands of miles to meet people? Even God sent his only begotten Son so he could be face to face with mankind. These meetings might not always under the friendliest of terms, but at the end of the day the potential for friendship becomes significantly greater. Throughout my Army career I have faced numerous instances of conflict. Guess how many of those same instances were resolved face to face? Most all of them. Every situation may have not ended in the best of friends, but a ground of respect had been laid. After all, is this not what most people seek after when it comes to relationships? Simply, to be respected for who they are and what they are called to do.

God does not call Christians to be doormats. We have a responsibility to live up to not only Biblical ethics, but the ethics that are preached by the organizations that we work for. The Army has preached throughout my time in the service that each soldier has the right to be treated with dignity and respect. There are those who often cross that line and when they do it is our individual responsibility to confront the offender with the offense. If we fail to do so we are only hurting ourselves as resentment and bitterness festers. These types of environments are kind of like the moron Drill Sergeant who threw a can of CS gas into a third floor room when my mask was broke and I found myself quickly not being able to breath.

Anytime I found myself on the receiving end of disrespect it was like the CS gas invaded my space once again cutting off my oxygen supply. I just have to get out of the room! I must find air and the situation must be addressed. I am not sure what was going on in the life of our Command Sergeant Major on the arsenal, but he had opened one too many cans of CS in my presence. I repeatedly felt disrespected in his presence and I had enough. So, I requested a face to face meeting with him. He made me schedule an appointment with his secretary even though we worked in the same office which irritated me even more. Nevertheless, the appointment was scheduled.

When we met I explained to him why I felt disrespected and ask if there was anything that I did to personally offend him. He stated that I did not personally offend him and would not go into a great deal of why he acted in the manner that he did. The important end state of our conversation was this- a new ground of respect was laid. At the end of the meeting, we shook hands and went back to our business. This would not have occurred on a telephone, fakebook, email, or in any other manner than face to face. I could write a book alone where the pages would be filled up with these stories that I have experienced throughout my career as a soldier.

Do Not Follow Me!

Isaiah 55:11 So shall my word be that goeth forth out of my mouth: it shall not return unto me void, but it shall accomplish that which I please, and it shall prosper in the thing whereto I sent it.

We all want our voices heard, especially when it pertains to our faith. If there are 1000 people in a burning building we want all 1000 to hear our voices so they can all be guided to safety. When I take time to share the Word of God and my experiences as a Christian on the net, I want God's Word and these experiences to go viral. Well, I have mostly been on social media since 2008 and have played around with the internet years prior. I have yet to personally see a Bible verse, devotion, or sermon go viral. As for my other various thoughts, I have had only one thought go viral on the net in 2012 after the December 14, 2012 Newtown massacre.

Evil does not exist within a gun.
It exists in the minds and hearts of those
who pull the trigger for evil purposes.

This post was shared hundreds of thousands of times on the internet after I initially shared it on The Soldier's Sanctuary Fakebook Page we had, and which you can see its viral presence even today by a simple Google search of the quote. That post and all other posts were deleted or hidden when I decided to lock myself out of that page and others. I had a different internet handle at the time, so few if any were able to "follow" my internet traffic thereafter.

I had to evaluate my internet presence and return on investment. Was the time invested aligning with the pure intention of the presence? When it pertains to the Word of God which is the purest of intentions we can have, I have to continually revert to Isaiah 55:11 knowing that God's Word will not return void and that even if one person is helped without us even knowing it, our time is well invested.

The problem begins to fester when our intentions begin to lack purity which leads our attention to become unbalanced. Instead of focusing on the few who are blessed and helped by the Word of God we share, we become focused on who is following us instead of the few we are helping to follow God. This reminds me of the struggle between David and Saul when they too fell to the same numbering allure.

1 Samuel 18:7 And the women answered one another as they played, and said, Saul hath slain his thousands, and David his ten thousands.

In essence, the women provided the "likes" while David and Saul monitored the numbers for their own personal glory. David later repents of these actions.

1 Samuel 24:10 And David's heart smote him after that he had numbered the people. And David said unto the LORD, I have sinned greatly in that I have done: and now, I beseech thee, O LORD, take away the iniquity of thy servant; for I have done very foolishly.

Over the years, when my attention becomes unaligned with true intention I must step back and reevaluate both, even if it means locking myself out of a social media account or deleting it all together. This is why I have posted as a continual reminder- I am not looking for followers, I am looking for others to follow Jesus with me.

I have also come to the point of despising the whole social media numbering system that appeals to the flesh and I refuse to subject myself to the laughable popularity contest the numbering system propagates, especially when many of these sites are dominated by bot followers that have been purchased. Now, as I maintain this blog I have arrived to the understanding that if no one else visits the site that is alright with me. Why? Because at the very least I am being blessed as I type away for the glory of God. He speaks to me during this time of writing and thought process. Therefore, even if it just I that is helped, His Word does not return void.

On a side note, I do believe I will be inserting this somewhere within "A Soldier's Progress," even though my plan is to expand upon this topic in a separate book. Also, this site is now my social media where there are no public "Followers" and I am starting over from scratch. Readers can keep up with this blog by an RSS feed or by subscribing above. Even so, do not follow me. Follow Jesus!

HOLY BEARD!

Not to sure how "Holy" my beard is, but I do consider it to be a holy experience. For 22 years I shaved for the Army and could not wait until retirement when I could finally grow one. I had absolutely no idea what the beard was going to look like, but when the time came my mug was going to grow something. I signed out for terminal leave in February 2016 and immediately began to grow my beard. During the second week of May I decided to attempt to trim it up myself and ended up jacking it up! So, I shave it all off! Back to day zero! My wife was happy, but not I. I felt like I was stripped down to my underwear and was forced to run around naked in public.

Today, I was in some rather high winds and decided to capture the wind whip my beard in the air. You want to know what is feels like? Freedom! And this freedom is completely tied to my spirituality. Every time my wife tells me I need to shave off my beard, my return reply is, "It is Spiritual!" Then I proceed to tell her that the Bible is more for beards than it is not. Now, she really does not like the beard and holds her breath when she speaks of it; but, she loves me and bears with it...only because she loves me.

Are beards Biblical? Absolutely! Most of the men recorded in the Bible had beards to include Jesus for starters. It seems to have been shameful not to have a beard.

A Soldier's Progress

2 Samuel 10:5 When they told it unto David, he sent to meet them, because the men were greatly ashamed: and the king said, Tarry at Jericho until your beards be grown, and then return.

No wonder, I felt naked after I shaved the beard I messed up when I first retired! It seems though that our culture has the beard phenomenon in reverse. Many act as if it is a shame to have a beard. I am telling you, a beard is spiritual and it is hard to explain!

I did not know how my beard would turn out since the last time that I tried to grow any significant facial hair was when I was a teenager prior to enlisting in the Army. You can Google the outcome of those attempts with one phrase- Shaggy from Scooby Doo. Also, during periods of leave I would grow what I could, but it still was not enough to tell me how a full beard would look. Not to mention, my Dad told me a couple of times that he could not grow a full beard.

Psalms 133:2 It is like the precious ointment upon the head, that ran down upon the beard, even Aaron's beard: that went down to the skirts of his garments;

Right now it has been a year and seven months since I last shaved. I have had a few trims on the sides, but that is about it. When my beard was shorter within the first year I was not that impressed with the way it looked. I read where bearded men stated over and over, "Wait and Be Patient." So, I have waited and I do believe my patience is paying off. I am happy about my beard's growth and progress. On another note, while I am happy with the progress of my beard, I am happy that my sons are doing some shaving for a few years also while they are serving in the Army.

Children's Continue Service

As I complete this book I am proud to write about my two oldest sons who are currently serving in the Army and even earned advanced rank during their enlistments for achieving the rank of Eagle Scout in the Boy Scouts. Judah who is our oldest son and Jesse who is our second oldest, only ten months apart, have considered the Army ever since they were able to speak and walk. They would play Army and I even had the work on their push-ups. It seems if I remember correctly they could accomplish around thirty push-ups with correct form by the time they reached kindergarten.

As they grew I reminded them about their interest and the wise decision to serve if they were able. I told them that if they decided to join they needed to complete at least one term of service and decide if they wanted to make a career out of the Army or not and that there was no sense in doing more than one term if they were not going to go all the way to retirement. A second or third term without retirement would only result in missed time and experience in the civilian world.

I am very proud of each of our children to include our daughter and youngest son. Each of them have achieved academic excellence and have sought after clear established goals in their lives. Our youngest son is not continuing with the Scouts due to recent policy changes, but he is following in the footsteps of our oldest sons with Wrestling. Regardless of where this life leads for our children I simply want them to seek the will of God for their lives daily. I want them to seek God to overcome any and all obstacles and stigmas that may come into their paths. Speaking of stigmas...

Conquered Stigmas

Prior to leaving for Basic Training in 1994 there seemed to be a stigma upon military service within the church community I was involved with after becoming a Christian in 1993. The thought pattern associated with a Christian serving in the military consisted of stumbling and roadblocks. Many thought the idea of joining the military was the end of Christian growth period.

Matthew 8:8-10 The centurion answered and said, Lord, I am not worthy that thou shouldest come under my roof: but speak the word only, and my servant shall be healed. For I am a man under authority, having soldiers under me: and I say to this man, Go, and he goeth; and to another, Come, and he cometh; and to my servant, Do this, and he doeth it. When Jesus heard it, he marvelled, and said to them that followed, Verily I say unto you, I have not found so great faith, no, not in Israel.

Now that I am retired after 22 years of service, I am

considered to be a veteran. I have noticed and continue to learn that there is an existing stigma concerning veterans too. One day on a job that I worked at just after retiring I was speaking to an employee of a hospital that I was contracted to work at. In the conversation I mentioned that I had just retired from the Army and the employee responded, "You don't have any mental issues do you?" I kindly replied that military service does not equate to mental issues. I believe the employee could sense my irritation, even though I was attempting to be gently informative, because the employee immediately attempted to retract the statement by "clarifying."

Stigmas often exist because of past experiences and knowledge of a certain level of truth contained within the stigma. For instance, do Christians join the service and experience challenges with their faith? Of course, and some falter too. Are there veterans who have milked the VA system by erroneously claiming they have physical and mental disabilities that do not exist or are grossly exaggerated so they can get a welfare check? Sure! I see it all the time and hear the stories myself and realize the fraud is the same that is seen is the Social Security system. But, we are talking about a large sum of people and anytime you are dealing with a large sum of people you are going to find a certain number within the sum who fuel misguided stigmas with their careless behavior.

There are countless soldiers and veterans who are doing good on and off the battlefield who are undeserving of such stigmas. I am thankful for those who really appreciate our military and veterans, knowing that there will always be those who abuse the system and life and general, so that those who deserve the thanks do not go without thanks. There are many veterans who are in genuine need of assistance and I hate the abusive behavior of some who call themselves veterans and make the veteran community look bad.

Now I want to speak of Conquering Stigmas. Since the day of my salvation, by the power and grace of God, I have sought to conquer the stigma of Christians serving in the military. You would think that the testimony of the Centurion would be enough. After all, Jesus stated that he had the greatest faith in all of Israel in Matthew 8. This alone tells us that a Christian can serve in the military while at the same time exercise great faith. My memoir, "A Soldier's Progress" highlights many of the opportunities I had to exercise my faith while on active duty and while serving with The Soldier's Sanctuary. As a veteran, these opportunities continue.

Just yesterday, I had the privilege and honor to sit with two other veterans and study the Bible during our men's Bible study. We discussed the faith of Noah and how he followed the instructions from God step by step and how important it is to focus on each step that God gives versus attempting to decipher and figure the end state of the project that we are assigned to. So many steps are often missed when we make this mistake. Then we talked about some of the recent steps of faith we had experienced.

Ray talked about how he was able to help a veteran family in need by filling up a couple of carts of groceries this past Thanksgiving and showing up to their house with bags of groceries. The family was so thankful and their hearts were touched. As Ray was at the house he noticed the family's dogs, so the next day he showed up with some more bags of groceries unannounced. The bags were filled with dog food and treats. We spoke of Shawn's blog that he invests in for the veteran community who suffer with moral injuries and how Biblical men to include David overcame their own moral injuries. Shawn also serves at a veteran non-profit as a chef.

The point is this, yesterday there were three veterans seeking God for the strength to take the steps of faith that are required to not only conquer unwarranted stigmas, but sin as well. These two veterans that I had the blessing to fellowship and worship with yesterday is what it is all about. We draw strength from one another, we learn from each other, and we conquer stigmas together by the grace of God and the Name of Jesus. If these types of stigmas can be conquered within our adjacent units called church, just think all that can be accomplished for the glory of our God and Savior!

Adjacent Units

As an Infantryman, I have participated in many operations orders which are detailed instructions and plans for a military mission. In Ranger training the details were so precise that the operation orders could take over 2 hours to pitch to fellow soldiers. Instructions such as rotate your rucksack off of your non-firing arm, place in cat eyes up (illumination tape,) with you rifle pointing towards the 12 o'clock are just a few of the very detailed micro instructions during Ranger training for the individual soldier.

These small details were important to memorize so that nothing would be missed. Without the accomplishment of the small micro details the macro instructions would never be accomplished. One of these macro instructions was adjacent unit coordination and/or friendly unit coordination. This is where a unit lets other units to the front, rear, and sides know what is going on with their mission and what to expect. This type of coordination can ultimately prevent friendly fire.

When I hit the ground and our current Army retirement location, one of the first things I attempted to accomplish was adjacent/friendly unit coordination. I called and emailed like minded churches in our area to see if I could set up a meeting to let the know that The Soldier's Sanctuary was in the area. I was hoping to see if there was any way that we could work together for the Kingdom. After all, as Christians we so have the same macro mission do we not? Granted, the micro details may differ greatly. As I have said many times, "God's will for each of our lives is as unique as our fingerprints" But, for the sake of unity and cohesiveness there are ways that churches can work together on the macro level to prevent friendly fire and for the glory of God.

Psalms 133:1 Behold, how good and how pleasant it is for brethren to dwell together in unity!

Well, unfortunately...none of the churches replied to my calls or emails. I know that church staffs are busy, at least I hope so, but I could not even get a Christian greeting in reply. Not even a "hey bro, welcome to our community! We are extremely busy at the moment, but will try to schedule a meeting with you soon." Nope, not a single reply. There is only one conclusion for this type of response. These churches do not value The Soldier's Sanctuary as an adjacent or friendly unit. These type of careless responses can only mean that they view us as a threat.

We are in a Spiritual War and we need each other. The problem is when we begin to treat people as resources (machines) for personal kingdom building, instead of soldiers of Christ who are all fighting the same battle for the Kingdom of God. The problem with this is the "machines" are dwindling in number which is stressing the Commercial Church. Therefore, when a new church enters a community they are deemed a threat against existing resources or what the Commercial Church would say, "market share."

The New Testament church has nothing to gain and nothing to lose. It lost and gained everything when Jesus Christ became the Commander and Chief. We, the New Testament Church, have one mission and one fight. I really do realize this and hope one day some of these churches will embrace this ideology and start coordinating with their adjacent units for the Kingdom of God instead of ignoring them for the kingdoms of men.

EPILOGUE

A Soldier's Progress will continue until the day I meet the LORD face to face.

1 Corinthians 13:12 KJV — For now we see through a glass, darkly; but then face to face: now I know in part; but then shall I know even as also I am known.

You are more than welcome to continue following this story and journey at

https://www.youtube.com/c/ASoldiersProgress

https://www.facebook.com/soldiersprogress

<u>I AM</u>

I am a sinner.

Romans 3:23 For all have sinned, and come short of the glory of God;

I am unable to afford the price for my sin.

Romans 6:23 For the wages of sin is death; but the gift of God is eternal life through Jesus Christ our Lord.

I am grateful that Jesus paid that price and God has offered this payment as a free gift.

John 3:16 For God so loved the world, that he gave his only begotten Son, that whosoever believeth in him should not perish, but have everlasting life.

1 John 5:11 And this is the record, that God hath given to us eternal life, and this life is in his Son. 12 He that hath the Son hath life; and he that hath not the Son of God hath not life. 13 These things have I written unto you that believe on the name of the Son of God; that ye may know that ye have eternal life, and that ye may believe on the name of the Son of God.

John 14:6 Jesus saith unto him, I am the way, the truth, and the life: no man cometh unto the Father, but by me.

I am certain I will spend eternity with our God and maker, thus escaping a Godless Hell.

John 3:36 He that believeth on the Son hath everlasting life: and he that believeth not the Son shall not see life; but the wrath of God abideth on him.

John 1:12 But as many as received him, to them gave he power to become the sons of God, even to them that believe on his name: 13 Which were born, not of blood, nor of the will of the flesh, nor of the will of man, but of God.

I am saved.

Romans 10:9 That if thou shalt confess with thy mouth the Lord Jesus, and shalt believe in thine heart that God hath raised him from the dead, thou shalt be saved. 10 For with the heart man believeth unto righteousness; and with the mouth confession is made unto salvation. 11 For the scripture saith, Whosoever believeth on him shall not be ashamed. 12 For there is no difference between the Jew and the Greek: for the same Lord over all is rich unto all that call upon him. 13 For whosoever shall call upon the name of the Lord shall be saved.

I am truly a recipient of God's grace.

Ephesians 2:8 For by grace are ye saved through faith; and that not of yourselves: it is the gift of God: 9 Not of works, lest any man should boast.

I am a soldier of Jesus Christ.

2 Timothy 2:3-4 Thou therefore endure hardness, as a good soldier of Jesus Christ. No man that warreth entangleth himself with the affairs of this life; that he may please him who hath chosen him to be a soldier.

I am what I am because of the great and Almighty- I AM.

John 8:58 Jesus said unto them, Verily, verily, I say unto you, Before Abraham was, I AM.

Simple Prayer of Salvation:

Father Lord Jesus,

You are a merciful, loving, gracious, holy, and glorious God. I know that I am a sinner in need of your forgiveness and grace. Forgive me o'LORD. Thank you for your great sacrifice on the cross and showing the world your Divinity by rising from the dead so that I and others may have life. May you lead and guide me for the remainder of my days for your honor and glory. Thank you my LORD, GOD, and SAVIOR.

In Jesus Name I pray. Amen

A Soldier's Progress

BONUS: TAKE AWAY THOUGHTS

A Marriage Note to Self

I have been to churches where I have
seen many pious beaver cleavers
But it seems more than not they
only prove to be overdressed deceivers

Marriage is not a pious front of perfection
It is a commitment that endures the trials of
life without defection

The marriage that endures does not come
without cost, if you are foolish to think so
all will be lost.

Love is the currency and self-sacrifice is the
work. If regular deposits are made there will
be no desire for other accounts to lurk.

No, our marriage has not arrived and it is not to
be a trophy on a shelf, these words just happen
to be a marriage note to self.

June 23, 2018

Evil does not exist within a gun.
It exists in the minds and hearts
of those who pull the trigger for
evil purposes.

Governments can free the body;
however, they have no power to
free the soul and spirit. Providence
holds the keys of absolute freedom.
Lest we forget, In God We Trust!

What is truth? The Word is Truth.
What type of response should
the truth invoke? Visit Plato's
Cave, even he understood the
rightful behavior of those loosed
from the chains of ignorance.

Since when have so many become
concerned for the livelihood of the
little ones when millions have been
slaughtered annually before they
even cross the border of the womb?

All I know is, if God can create all
existence and govern the same with
physical laws that only he can transcend,
he can with ease address and resolve
our daily woes.

A Soldier's Progress

One of Satan's greatest weapons
employed against humanity is
Moral Injury. The Centurion who
was tasked to scourge and crucify
our LORD could have easily fell to
this destructive weapon, but he did
not. He conquered it through Jesus
Christ!

The will of God for each of our lives
is as unique as our fingerprints.

Ideas are seeds planted in the
gardens of faith. The significant
question pertains to the sower.
Who is planting these ideas and
where does the seed originate?
A blind answer can only sprout
the weeds of of death.

Evil is never satisfied until it
achieves death. Its gradual
progress is a moral decay that
erodes life and society. It seeks
more destructive drugs, depraved
sex, and unchecked ambition in
order to reach its destructive
end-state and anti-God agenda.

If it was not for the love, patience,
and consolation of our LORD and
God we would all be crushed like
bugs. Thankfully, God even
protects us from our own stupidity.

Evil Ideologies are much like
flies that gravitate towards
the stench of death. No wonder
so many feed upon the dying
platforms of race and identity
politics. All I know is that the
platform I preach never dies.

Beware of Puppet Masters who
control men with religious strings
and extortion. Toilet paper has
more worth than their pious titles
and will bring a greater return on
investment.

At some point the self-pity panties
need to come off and the Armor of
God needs to be put on. God has a
plan for you and me and his will for
each of our lives is as unique as
our fingerprints.

A Soldier's Progress

Legalism and License are results of
the Mammon structure, ideology,
and methodology of the Commercial
Church. Each are necessary for the
purpose of control and domination
of the sheeple market share.
Legalism feeds the sheep that worship
men and license feeds the sheep that
worship themselves.

Prayer is how the soul
breathes. It is the new
born's first cry. No
breath equals no life.

Many assemble for a
personality found in a
man, few assemble
for The Personality of
Jesus Christ found in
God.

LF6, why do you preach under a
pseudonym? Because we are living in
a day where Mammon priests are
pimping the name of our LORD Jesus
to make a name for themselves. Do
not worry about who I am, worry about
who He is. I will fail you, you will fail me,
Jesus will never fail us.

The average man has a
care meter that has the
blast radius of a hand
grenade. So, if you are
depending on an appropriate
reciprocation and appreciation
for your time and effort from
man do not hold your breath.
Just do it for God.

Any type of sex outside
of the marriage of one
man and one woman is
just a cheap imitation
that will never satisfy the
soul. It comes with a
great cost that breaks
the heart and spirit.

A wounded dog backed
in a corner will bite. Focus
on the wound and not the
bite and a great friend will
be obtained.

Die for convictions and leave
ambiguity upon the wrestling
mat and in the coffee shop.

A Soldier's Progress

I do not know the genie-jesus,
dashboard-jesus, bling-jesus,
muslim-jesus, jw-jesus,
mormon-jesus, or your
personal ready whip jesus.
I only know the LORD
Jesus Christ, so quit
introducing them to me.

There is a short distance between
Heaven and Hell. It is roughly 18 inches,
which is the distance between your head
and your heart. Head knowledge alone
will not save anyone. Even the devils
simply acknowledge Christ with no
further action.

At the White Throne Judgment:
LORD, why should I be cast into Hell?
Don't you know who I am! Have you
not seen my total follower count on
social media!?

I am not looking for followers, I am
looking for others to follow Jesus
with me.

Nothing else matters, but the will
of God!

LF6 Memoir

It is never a matter of
losing your salvation,
it is a matter of being
saved in the first place.

Where are our Christian men?
On the sidelines of life
castrated by Satan while the
women pick up the slack.
Men, get your Spiritual Balls
back!

I will fail you, you will fail me,
Jesus will never fail us!

FAMILY PHOTO APPENDIX

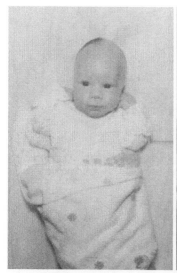

A Soldier's Progress

This is the LORD'S
doing; it is marvellous
in our eyes.

Psalms 118:23

A Soldier's Progress

Made in the USA
Monee, IL
04 November 2019